Struggle and Lose, Struggle and Win

Struggle and Lose, Struggle and Win:

The United Mine Workers

Elizabeth Levy
Tad Richards

Photo Essay by Henry E. F. Gordillo

Four Winds Press, New York

Library of Congress Cataloging in Publication Data
Levy, Elizabeth.
  Struggle and lose, struggle and win.
  Bibliography: p.
  Includes index.
  Summary: Traces the history of the United Mine Workers, the first major
industry-wide union, emphasizing its struggles to organize, win improved
conditions for its members, and rid itself of internal corruption.
    1. United Mine Workers of America—History.   2. Trade-unions—Coal-
miners—United States—History.   [1. United Mine Workers of America—
History.   2. Labor unions—History.   3. Coal mines and mining—History]
I. Richards, Tad, joint author.   II. Gordillo, Henry E. F.   III. Title.
HD6515.M615L48   331.88′11′622330973   76-56703
ISBN 0-590-07355-9

Published by Four Winds Press
A Division of Scholastic Magazines, Inc., New York, N.Y.
Copyright © 1977 by Elizabeth Levy
Printed in the United States of America
Library of Congress Catalog Card Number: 76-56703
81 80 79 78 77
  5 4 3 2 1

Contents

Photo Essay

by

Henry E. F. Gordillo

These photographs were taken at a mine that is only three feet high. Miners work on their stomachs all through their shift. The coal is taken by truck and conveyor belt down the mountain to the machinery that breaks it up into smaller lumps before it is loaded into railway cars.

Henry E. F. Gordillo

Dawn shift—miners on flat cars.

Testing safety lamp.

Miners receiving work orders. Entrance to mine seen at right.

Coal hopper loader.

Miner.

Strip mining—mountain cut away to reach coal seam.

Company store.

House (not deserted).

Graveyard.

Family.

Coal truck driver.

Dawn.

Struggle and Lose, Struggle and Win

1: King Coal and His Servants

It's dark as a dungeon, and damp as the dew
Where the dangers are double, and the
        pleasures are few
Where the rain never falls, and the sun
        never shines
It's dark as a dungeon, down in the mine.
        Merle Travis
        copyright 1947, American Music Inc.

America is so rich in coal that it makes the Arab nations seem energy poor. This coal is not only energy. It has been used to make such varied products as sulfa drugs, nylon, plastic, aspirin and perfume.

Coal is made by the earth's pressure squeezing the oxygen and hydrogen out of woody fiber until the carbon molecules combine into black chunks. North America has such an abundance of wooded areas that coal runs below our hills like black rivers. It is estimated that in North America there are nearly 5 trillion metric tons of coal, while in the United States alone it is estimated that we have enough coal to last twenty-five hundred years. Contrast this with dwindling oil reserves, and the old statement, "coal is king," takes new life.

There are significant coal fields all across the country, from the East Coast to the Midwest, the Rockies, and the Pacific Coast. Coal is found in twenty-five states, but the largest fields are in the Appalachian coal area, ranging from Alabama north to Pennsylvania and Ohio.

Long before coal was mined in the Appalachian hills, the

region was the home for countless poor, uneducated, and desperate people. They had first come to the United States in the seventeenth and eighteenth centuries, when the rich plantation owners of the South could not get enough slaves to work their cotton fields. The English Parliament passed laws that enabled the plantation owners to pay the passage for poor people—often from orphanages and debtors' prisons—from English and Irish cities to come to America in exchange for seven years free labor. But once they arrived many of these immigrants, called indentured servants, escaped to the foothills of Kentucky and Tennessee, to be joined later by those whose period of servitude was over.

Because these immigrants came from cities, they knew little about farming. Unlike the middle-class pilgrims who came to New England, the settlers of Appalachia didn't even know how to read or write. They had few skills to pass on to their children, and managed to survive on the game they shot and the vegetables they managed to raise. But most of them didn't prosper, and few of them ever would.

In the 1870s the railroads pressed into the hills of Appalachia, and gangs of black workers laid down the tracks that would provide a way to get the coal, so abundant in the region, to the steel mills and other industries. It was at this point that coal mining began in earnest in Appalachia and there was a pressing need for men to work the mines. Many blacks from the railroad gangs stayed to become coal miners, and the descendants of the original indentured servants came down from the hills and into the mines. Yet, the demand for coal was so great, and the coal fields so rich, that even more men were needed.

The coal mine operators employed labor agents to go to

Europe to find more men to work the mines. These new immigrants came from Italy, Hungary, Poland, and Greece, and very few could speak English. Their transportation was paid by the coal and steel companies. After going through immigration at Ellis Island, they were quickly loaded onto trains and carried to the southern coal fields. Mixed in with these immigrants from southern and eastern Europe, were men from Wales or England who had experience in the mines of Britain. Most of these miners came to America seeking new hope, but mining was the only kind of work they knew. They wanted a new life, but they ended up back in the mine.

In the nineteenth century, there were no laws regulating the working conditions of the miners. Miners were paid by the load of coal, not by the number of hours or days that they worked. Any work which did not directly produce usable coal was considered "dead work," and the miners were not paid for it. Dead work included drilling holes to prepare for blasting, checking and repairing damage to the timbers that held up the roofs of their coal room, clearing away debris caused by the blasting that loosened the coal, breaking through walls with pick and ax to set up a new coal room, clearing away rocks and debris from the tracks along which traveled the mine cars that carried the coal, and washing the coal before it left the mine to remove rock, slate, and other impurities. The miner was paid for none of that difficult and time-consuming work.

It was the owners' contention that coal miners were independent contractors, much like gold prospectors, and therefore all the difficulties attending the removal of coal from the ground were the miners' concern, not the owners'.

But the miners' independence ended when it came to

the selling of the coal. The coal they mined belonged to the owner of the mine they had been working. The owner set the price, and even was allowed to estimate how much coal was in a load. The price was as low as two cents for an 80-pound bushel. The coal was weighed by the owner's men, and the miners weren't allowed to watch. Many miners ended up with less than a dollar for a full day's work.

Child labor was another common practice. Boys of nine or ten, sometimes even younger, were put to work separating the coal from the slate as it moved through on conveyor belts. The coal frequently crushed their fingers, and many times a boy would fall exhausted onto the conveyor belt and be crushed to death by the oncoming coal. Children were also used as "trap boys" to open the trap doors in the mines for the mules to pass through. This job required that they sit alone in a dark passageway of the mine for twelve hours a day.

Most of the coal mines were in unpopulated regions and workers had to be brought to them. Housing was built for the miners by the operators on company-owned land. The company owned all the houses, the health facilities, the stores, even the churches. The company controlled all rents, and all prices at the store. Through these means, the company could make sure that the workers were always in debt to the company.

There was no way out of this maze for the miner. He needed a job, so he worked in the mines. The company saw to it that his rent and food were more than he could afford so he borrowed money on next week's pay. The company eventually got back all the money they paid out in wages through high rents and high prices at their stores. Their workers were thus never able to leave the company, and could never demand more money or better working conditions because they were always in debt.

Sometimes an independent store would open near a company town and the store owner would charge prices much lower than those of the company store. In order to discourage their miners from using those stores, some companies paid their workers in "scrip"—coupons redeemable only at the company store—instead of cash. In many respects, the workers in a company town were like serfs, virtual economic prisoners of the mine operators.

These intolerable conditions were not limited to the coal mines of Appalachia. Coal miners from all over America have faced much the same problems—dangerous working conditions, low pay, economic bondage to their jobs, child labor, lack of health care for work-related diseases and the destruction of their environment by irresponsible mining techniques. Some of these conditions have been cleared up by legislation and union pressure over the years; others are as bad or worse today as they were a hundred years ago.

In the early days, a miner walked into the mine lighting his way with an open-flame carbide lamp fastened to a soft canvas and leather miner's cap. The lamps often caught fire in the coal dust. The hats provided no protection from cave-ins. Some of the early mines used primitive electrically powered cutting machines to cut the coal, but most of the work was done with picks.

The miner strapped thick rubber pads to his knees and began to pick at the coal until he had cleared a strip as far as his pick handle would allow. Then he would put a stick of dynamite into the hole he had dug and move out of the way for the powder to blow. Then he would go back and pile the coal into cars, most of which were driven by mules or horses, although the mine locomotives made an early appearance.

Modern mines are much different, but one thing never changes. It is always "dark as a dungeon down in the mine." In the mines of today, an elevator takes the miner into the earth. At the bottom of the elevator shaft, coal trains take the men through dark tunnels, dimly lit. Sometimes they ride for six miles. When they get off the train, the water is often up to their ankles. The light on their caps cuts the darkness just a little. The modern miner doesn't have to use a pick and ax. He uses a labor-saving device called a continuous mining machine that cuts the coal from the face of the wall, crunches it into chunks, and deposits it onto a shuttle car. The machine creates an overpowering noise in the tiny space in which the miner has to operate. As it works the machine throws up an incredible cloud of coal dust into the stale, musty air the miner has to breathe. A man who spends his working days breathing in rock and coal dust develops debilitating diseases that attack the lungs. The most deadly of these, "black lung," has only recently been recognized as an occupational disease of miners. Many owners and operators still fight bitterly against paying health and disability benefits for black lung, yet it has been estimated that black lung adds another thousand deaths to the annual mine fatality count in Pennsylvania alone. In 1975, a Columbus, Ohio, grand jury indicted the Consolidation Coal Company for falsifying dust samples submitted to government inspectors so that they would appear not to contain enough coal dust to cause black lung diseases, when in fact, the coal dust level was way above government safety standards.

The mining of coal creates a tremendous amount of

waste material, for coal is embedded in surrounding rock that has no value to industry. There are two basic methods of coal mining today—strip-mining and deep-mining. In strip-mining, the coal is dug from the surface with great earth-moving machines. Hilltops are torn off in huge chunks, the coal is shaken loose, and the refuse is littered over the countryside, killing vegetation, polluting the waters, leaving raw, gaping scars. Recently some coal companies have tried to restore and replant the hills they have destroyed by strip-mining, but it is too early to tell whether the damage they have caused is permanent.

In areas that are deep-mined, the refuse from the mines is piled on the surface, in huge, ugly smoking mountains of "slag" that pollute the air and water for miles around. In 1972, in Logan County, West Virginia, a slag heap dam on the Buffalo Creek collapsed, sending a roaring flood down into the valley below. Fourteen towns were destroyed, leaving 125 people dead and over 5,000 homeless. Experts determined that the accident was caused by negligence on the part of the Buffalo Creek Mining Company, but the company paid only a token $25 fine. The company did at first contribute to relief for the victims of the flood, but after the publicity surrounding the disaster died down, many families found it hard to get any relief at all. Miners were even denied back pay for the time lost from work because of the flood.

Since 1910, when the Bureau of Mines began keeping official statistics, over 114,000 men have been killed in American mines. Since 1930, when the first statistics on disabling injuries were compiled, more than 1,500,000 such injuries have been reported. The most common fatal accident in the mines is a cave-in. There is a sudden crack of supporting timber, and the miner has perhaps a split

second to scramble or crawl to safety, then the roof col-
lapses burying whatever and whomever is beneath it under
hundreds of tons of coal and rock and earth.

The second most common type of mine accident is an
explosion. When coal is separated from the surrounding
earth, methane gas is produced which is extremely ex-
plosive. To compound the danger, the fine coal dust produced by the machines can be ignited by a single spark.
In 1970, 38 men were killed in a mine explosion in Hyden,
Kentucky, that was attributed to unsafe and out-moded
blasting techniques that had long been illegal.

Of course, it is possible to make the mines reasonably
safe, but the costs are high. However, the mine owners
are not the only ones to blame for letting the dangerous
conditions continue. Often the Mine Workers union has
failed to push for safety measures because their imple-
mentations would mean lower pay and lower owner con-
tributions to the pension fund.

Today many of the worst abuses in mining are gone. But
the mine owners did not give in gracefully. Some miners
and their families were shot, clubbed, burned to death, and
starved when they tried to join together in a union. But
eventually miners did succeed in forming America's first
great industrial union, the United Mine Workers of
America.

The UMW was born out of bitter and bloody struggles
that claimed the lives of thousands of working men,
women, and children. For many years it was the largest and
strongest union in America. Some of its leaders were
idealists, some were leaders who compromised, and some
were corrupt. Some rose to tremendous power and influence, most notably John L. Lewis, who rivaled Franklin D.
Roosevelt in popularity and fame. Lewis was at different

times in his career both a great idealist and a great compromiser.

The United Mine Workers union has inspired respect, admiration and contempt. It has won material, legislative and philosophical reforms for all workers. It has also led the way in showing how a union can betray its members, even murder them, and its story deserves to be told.

2 : America's First Labor Unions

If you want higher wages let me tell you
    what to do
You got to talk to the workers in the shop
    with you,
You got to build you a union, got to build
    it strong
And if you all stick together boys, it won't
    be long
You get shorter hours . . .
Better working conditions . . .
Take the kids to the seashore.
Well, it ain't quite that easy, so I better
    explain. . . .
        Talking Union, by Almanac Singers
        copyright 1947, People's Songs

The first workers' organizations in America were small, local groups of skilled workmen. In 1768, a group of 20 tailors in New York City went on strike against their employers. They were journeymen—that is, skilled craftsmen who did not yet have shops of their own, but worked in the establishments of master tailors. Since there was no easy way of replacing them with men of equal skills, this small group was able to put pressure on the master tailors to meet their wage demands.

There were other strikes like this among other groups of craftsmen at this time, but there were not any real unions such as there are today, because the workers had no real organization. Every now and then, a group of men, all doing the same type of work, would refuse to work until a specific demand was met, but then the group members would lose contact with each other and go in separate ways. Bakers, seamen, shoemakers, printers, and carpenters were among the trades that exerted this kind of occasional group pressure.

This loose type of organization was the forerunner of the craft union, the union of a group of craftsmen who have their specialized skill in common, and use the difficulty of replacement as a bargaining point.

With the coming of the industrial revolution, however, there were more and more workers for whom this sort of union was not effective. Miners and factory workers could be easily trained and easily replaced—all the more easily because of the rising number of immigrants coming to America looking for a new life and work of any sort.

At the same time, all the mechanical inventions of the industrial revolution compounded the problems. Work which had always been "skilled" was now becoming "unskilled" because of technological advances. For example, power looms were invented that anyone could be taught to run, and weavers found that their wages were cut in half between 1840 and 1845. Mechanical typesetters had the same impact on the careers of journeymen printers.

At first the workers tried to fight the machines by proving they could do the work as well and as fast. There was the legendary John Henry, thought to be a black man on a work gang, who challenged the steam drill to a race digging a railroad tunnel through the side of the mountain around 1870. Nobody is quite sure whether John Henry really did exist, but the printers did have a real-life hero who challenged the mechanical typesetter to a race.

The champion of the typesetters was a woman named Minnie. She was a stunningly attractive platinum blonde from Nebraska, at that time the only woman journeyman printer in the Midwest—quite possibly in the entire country.

The race was held, and Minnie won. The machine was no match for her when it came to setting type. And unlike John Henry, who "laid down his hammer and died" after the strain of beating the steam drill, Minnie lived to set type another day. Until the day she retired, even with all the mechanical advances of the age of machines, a machine was never made that could set type faster than Minnie. She took them all on, and beat them all.

But there were few victories for the American working man and woman—and child—in those decades. It was the era that Mark Twain called the Gilded Age. Great new railroad systems linked up the far corners of the nation. New methods of making steel and iron meant that America's vast national resources were being tapped in a way never before dreamed of. New methods of mill and factory operation created an immense national wealth out of those resources.

And almost all of that wealth was going into the pockets of a very few. The millionaires were permitted to operate under the philosophy of "laissez-faire capitalism"—the theory that if you left business alone it would produce the greatest happiness for the greatest amount of people.

In theory, laissez-faire capitalism was not supposed to benefit only the rich. The "bible" of the theory, The Wealth of All Nations, was published by Adam Smith, in 1776. According to Smith, the economy of all nations is supposed to run like a game with one rule. Every individual is supposed to be free to do whatever will bring him or her the most money. The theory assumes that people will produce only what others will buy, and people will take jobs to make money so that they can buy what others are producing.

Therefore, the owner of a business was justified in paying the lowest wages anyone would take. The idea of workers banding together to demand higher wages for all was anathema to the theory because then workers would not be acting as individuals. However, the rich and privileged rarely acted as individuals; they often had family wealth behind them, and they frequently banded together in corporations. Nevertheless, they were outraged at the idea of any attempt to organize labor. Union organizers were fired by the companies they worked for and put on a blacklist so that nobody else would hire them. Unions, therefore, had to become secret societies in order to survive. The company owners hired spies to infiltrate their ranks, and the leaders of the secret societies were marked for firing or worse.

The first great strike against this new industrial order was the Railroad Strike of 1877. It wasn't organized by any union, but spread by word of mouth and nearly became this country's first and only national walkout.

The strike started when the Baltimore and Ohio Railroad cut wages to $1.50 a day for most workers. On July 16, 1877, in the town of Martinsburg, West Virginia, the workers went on strike and refused to allow the trains to move.

Railroad workers all across the country joined in this spontaneous walkout. State militiamen were called out to try to break the strikes. In Reading, Pennsylvania, National Guardsmen fired into a crowd and killed 11 people. More and more people poured into the streets to support the strikers. The next day the governor of Pennsylvania called in fresh troops. The new troops not only refused to join the old, but they took the side of the strikers. They told the guardsmen, "If you fire at the mob, we'll fire at you."

Throughout the last half of July 1877, the country seemed to be on the verge of a full-fledged Second American Revolution. CITY IN POSSESSION OF COMMUNISTS read the headline in *The New York Times*, referring to the city of Chicago, which almost fully supported the strikers. In Pittsburgh, 600 militiamen marched on the city and within five minutes killed 26 people. The enraged populace fought back with whatever weapons they could lay their hands on at home. They were given support by sympathetic home-town Pittsburgh militiamen. Together, they completely routed the troops, driving them out of town. It was open warfare of American against American. And with the Civil War still fresh in everyone's mind, it seemed a very real possibility that this was the start of a second civil war, this time pitting rich against poor.

But the strike only lasted for about two weeks, and then, under pressure from Federal troops, it died almost as quickly as it had begun. There was no central organization of strikers, and not even one strong spokesman or hero to press the demands of the workingman emerged. In fact, it was far from clear what the demands of the strikers were.

The whole class of industrial workers was so new, had sprung up so quickly, that there was still room for debate as to just what its place was in the American system. A short time before 1877, the majority of Americans had worked for themselves on small farms or in small businesses. Now, suddenly, there were millions who worked for others. The debate was whether or not America *should* have a majority who worked for others—a wage-earning class.

In 1877, it was not by any means accepted by all workers that they were destined to be "wage slaves" under the American system. Many workers did not merely want their pay restored. Even at two dollars a day, it was hard to keep a family from starving. An alternate theory to laissez-faire capitalism was socialism. There were many who believed in abolishing altogether the wage system and the idea of a working class. There were a few days in St. Louis, during the 1877 strike, when workers actually did seize control of the railroads. Instead of shutting them down by a strike, they ran the railroads, keeping up schedules and collecting fares, sharing the profits among themselves. Then, ironically, it was the bosses who fought to shut the railroads down.

America's first great national labor union was founded on the basis of opposition to the wage system, and with the goal of solidarity of all workers, skilled and unskilled alike. This was the Noble and Holy Order of Knights of Labor.

The Knights of Labor had been in existence since 1869, but for many years it was a tiny, secret organization with no national power, and it played no role in the upheaval of 1877. But in 1884, a spontaneous and successful strike against Jay Gould's Union Pacific Railroad forced Gould, a notorious foe of labor, to recognize the Knights as a legitimate union.

That victory set off a chain reaction of strikes, and of new-formed Knights of Labor assemblies. In one year the Knights increased from 71,326 total membership to 111,-395. By the following year, 1886, the membership had leaped to over 700,000.

The philosophy of the Knights of Labor was expressed in the slogan, "An Injury to One Is the Concern of All." They believed in the unity of all workers, and equality of the sexes and races. They had some concrete demands: an eight-hour day, health and safety legislation for the workingmen, an end to child labor, and an end to forced, unpaid labor by convicts in competition with free labor. But their goals went way beyond these. They dreamed of a classless society. They believed that monopoly was evil, and they supported government ownership of railroads, telephones, and telegraphs, a system which would lead some day to a cooperative society.

The Knights of Labor were in many ways a curious choice for standard bearers of the working class. The most curious thing about them was that they were, in theory, totally opposed to strikes. Their president, or Grand Master Workman, Terence V. Powderly, an idealist if something of a bumbler, believed that striking for limited objectives—higher pay, the eight-hour day, or whatever issue of the moment was being argued—implied an acceptance of the wage system as a whole. However, after the success of the strike against Jay Gould, the Knights became the rallying point for all the pent-up working-class discontent in America. Their leaders might preach all they wanted: workingmen had found an organization to bring them together, and most workers wanted concrete gains such as a higher wage—and they wanted them in their lifetime.

There were numerous strikes throughout the mid-Eighties, as workers in one part of the country after another went out on strike and joined the Knights of Labor. There was not a great deal of centralized control in the Knights. It was an umbrella for local workingmen's groups everywhere—and more importantly, for all kinds of workingmen, of all degrees of skill and specialization.

The degree to which labor was becoming organized on a national scale alarmed the business community, who feared the threat of communism. Although very few of labor's demands were actually being met, the big bosses talked as if labor's demands were driving them out of business.

However, the Knights of Labor were not able to sustain their position as a labor force. May 1886, the time of the infamous Haymarket Riot, was the beginning of the end for them, even though they had very little, if anything, to do with the riot. A rival union organization had started a movement for the eight-hour day, and had declared a national strike if the eight-hour day wasn't recognized by May 1, 1886. Powderly opposed the strike, but many members of the Knights of Labor supported it. Saturday, May 1, was normally a working day, but 80,000 men and women struck in Chicago alone. By May 3rd, the strike was still on, and the press treated it as if it were a revolution. On the afternoon of the 3rd, a clash between strikers and police resulted in the death of four strikers. A rally to protest police brutality was immediately scheduled for the next evening in Chicago's Haymarket Square.

The next night it rained, and only about 300 people showed up. The rally was about over when 180 mounted policemen showed up to break it up. Suddenly a bomb was thrown into the middle of the police ranks, killing 7 policemen and wounding 67. The police then opened fire into the crowd, killing 10 people and wounding more than 50. Although it was never determined who threw the bomb, 7 leaders of the anarchist group who had called the rally were arrested, tried, and sentenced to death for murder. A wave of anti-labor hysteria was touched off in the nation's newspapers, and the Knights of Labor, the largest labor organization, was the primary target.

At the same time, Jay Gould had ruthlessly suppressed a new strike over wages and union recognition, and the

Knights of Labor had been unable to make their gains stick. Spurred on by the rising anti-union sentiment that was being cultivated in the wake of Haymarket, employers fought to break the unions with all the weapons at their disposal. The following tactics were commonly used:

Lockouts: Shutting down mills or factories and locking all the workers out until they agreed not to join the union. The choice was starvation or submission.

Blacklists: Agreements among employers not to hire a worker who had been fired elsewhere.

Yellow dog contracts: Making workers sign an oath that they wouldn't join a union as a condition of employment. The contracts were called "yellow dog" because they made the worker feel like a coward—but it was either sign or be fired.

Convict labor: Using prisoners from state prisons as work gangs in competition with free labor.

Armed violence: The biggest employers hired private police forces such as the Pinkerton Detective Agency, and even private armies, trained and maintained by the companies. Jay Gould boasted, "I can hire half the working class to kill the other half."

The suppression worked. Strikes were broken all over the country. The Knights of Labor shrank as quickly as they had expanded. Where gains had been made, they were in many places lost. The post-Haymarket scaremongering turned public sentiment against the Knights, even though they were not responsible for the rally. Within two years, their membership dropped from over 700,000 to 200,000, and shortly after that the union died completely.

When the Knights of Labor died, the interest in a cooperative industrial society died too, as well as the idea of a union of all working people. The next important force— and for over fifty years the only important force—in the American union movement was the American Federation of Labor.

The AFL, founded in 1886, was a collection of unions for different skilled crafts. It ignored the easily replaced industrial worker, and concentrated on practical goals for workers who had skills employers needed. Their motto was "a fair's day wage for a fair day's work," which implied their willingness to accept a system where some men would always be wage earners. They concentrated on making the wage earner's life as good as possible.

In place of the visionary Knights came a new kind of trade unionism. Led by skilled workers, the American Federation of Labor took a completely different tack.

The AFL was led by Samuel Gompers of the Cigar Makers Union. He was brought up on the Lower East Side of New York, and his father was a radical, but Gompers wanted to build a practical American labor movement, with bread-and-butter goals.

Because it was so easy to replace one unskilled worker with another, Gompers concentrated on the skilled workers. His union organized each craft into a national trade union. These unions charged high dues and initiation fees because Gompers knew unions had to be strong to match the power of corporations. This businesslike approach helped them grow into solid unions, and they won for their members higher pay, shorter hours and better working conditions.

By 1890, only four years after its founding, the Federation was the central force in American labor. In the next twenty-five years, its workers' average weekly wages rose from $17.57 to $23.98 and the working week was cut from 54.4 to 48.9 hours.

Unfortunately, during the same time the AFL was winning such gains, mass production industries were making obsolete more and more of the old crafts and thereby creating many millions more unskilled workers. The mines, mills and railroads that were creating the industrial revolution employed hundreds of thousands of workers and most of them were unskilled and ignored by the AFL.

3: Early History of the United Mine Workers

Now some people say a man's made out of
    mud,
But a poor man's made out of muscle and
    blood,
Muscle and blood, skin and bones,
A mind that's weak and a back that's strong.
You load sixteen tons and what do you get?
Another day older and deeper in debt.
St. Peter don't you call me 'cause I can't go,
I owe my soul to the company store.
                    © Merle Travis
                    copyright 1947, American Music Inc.

Mining is basically an unskilled trade, and that is a problem that has plagued all attempts to organize miners. When many people need work, the owner of a mine can easily replace one man with another. The first recorded strike of miners occurred in 1842. The miners were quick to realize that their only hope lay in unity, but it was difficult to organize men who were close to starving.

In the 1860s the standard pay rate was two and a half cents for a bushel that weighed 80 pounds. The owners of the mines estimated that a fast man with a pick could mine 100 bushels a day, but the miners estimated that they could produce 50 bushels in a 15-hour day.

In 1867, the operators of the Eagle Colliery, a small mine in St. Clair, Pennsylvania, cut wages back to two cents a bushel and the miners went out on strike. They were led by John Siney, who had a family heritage of not backing down to authority. His father was an Irish tenant farmer run out of Ireland for daring to challenge the authority of the British landlords. Siney's family moved to England, and at the age of seven, he started working full time in a mill in Lancashire, England, which left him no time to go to school. In his mid-twenties, he sought a better life in America and arrived in Pennsylvania, where he took a job working in the Colliery.

When the Colliery tried to cut the price per bushel, Siney, who was a natural born orator, convinced the men he worked with that they could fight back. Five hundred workers joined him in a strike.

It was not a large strike, but it was effective and well-timed. The operators of the Eagle Colliery discovered that the larger companies would not support them in a lockout of workers, and they had to settle quickly, restoring the wage cuts.

It was an impressive victory for Siney and by 1869 he had expanded his original group of strikers into a union of 30 locals and 30,000 members—four-fifths of all the workers in the anthracite or hard coal fields. Siney was the first president of the union, called the Workingmen's Benevolent Association. In 1873, a nationwide Miner's National Association was formed, and Siney became president of that organization.

From 1868 to 1875, Siney's union struggled to establish itself as a bargaining power in the coal fields. Siney was not afraid to lead his miners out on strike. Scarcely a year went by without one, and a couple of them lasted for months. The miners discovered that in unity there was strength.

The coal operators organized too, proving that unity

with money behind it could be even more powerful. The leader of the coal operators was Franklin B. Gowen, who owned 10,000 acres of coal lands and was also president of the Reading Railroad.

Because he controlled both railroads and coal, Gowen was in a position of dictatorial power in the coal fields. In 1871, the third strike in as many years had brought both miners and operators to a position of willingness to compromise. The miners were penniless and starving, but the smaller, independent operators had exhausted their coal reserves. They were in danger of bankruptcy if the strike did not end soon. They announced their willingness to meet the strikers' terms.

Gowen was horrified. He didn't control any of the mines that were about to give in to the workers, but he was determined to stop the settlement. He believed that if the union were successful it would eventually threaten his mines. He announced that he was doubling the freight rates for coal on his railroads. Now, even if the operators gave in to the strikers and reopened their mines, they would not be able to afford to ship their coal anywhere. Gowen made it clear the rates would remain doubled as long as the union existed. The mines would have to stay closed until the workers capitulated, whether the operators wanted it or not.

Large sections of the public were outraged. Gowen was considered too high-handed by many editorialists, and there was a wave of sympathy for the strikers. People felt the miners had a right to live decently. In Pennsylvania, a state senate committee was formed to investigate the legality of Gowen's decision to raise freight rates.

Then, just as public opinion seemed about to force Gowen to back down, suddenly the newspapers were filled with reports of the legendary, feared Molly Maguires, a clandestine terrorist organization. The Molly Maguires were supposed to be a secret army of Irish-American coal miners who engaged in organized guerrilla warfare against mine owners and also against mine workers who refused to join the union. The name and reputation of the Molly Maguires has lived on, like those of the SLA, IRA, Hell's Angels or Viet Cong, as a perversely romantic but basically frightening force in the middle of a peaceful society. The image of the Mollies is that of a band of outlaws fighting society's injustice with terror. The Mollies have made their imprint as memorable figures in history far more strongly than either John Siney or Franklin B. Gowen.

But it is not at all clear that the Mollies ever really existed. In fact, it seems much more likely that there never were any Molly Maguires. Certainly, there was plenty of violence on both sides in the coal fields, and certainly men were killed, but whether in fact there was a secret organized death squad is a moot point.

The man who unveiled the secret of the Molly Maguires to the world was Franklin B. Gowen. Suddenly public opinion changed from sympathy to fear and dread when people began to read about the militant Molly Maguires. It is possible that Gowen created the myth of the Mollies knowing what public reaction would be. The strikers were no longer sympathetic figures to the public, they were a murderous bunch of Irishmen with no respect for American values.

In fact, the Irish were the dominant ethnic group among the Pennsylvania miners, and many Irish miners were members of a secret fraternal organization called the Ancient Order of Hibernians. The members of the Hibernians shared a nostalgic memory of the Old Country and a common dissatisfaction with the lot of the Irish laborer in the coal fields. The Molly Maguires were supposed to be a secret organization composed of a select group of Hibernians. But no concrete evidence of the Mollies' existence— no correspondence, no membership lists, no memoirs or reminiscences or deathbed confessions by old ex-Mollies— has ever turned up.

The only evidence that has ever come to light about the Molly Maguires was gathered by the Pinkerton Detective Agency, hired by Gowen to infiltrate and expose the Mollies, and many historians now believe there never was any organization to expose. Instead, the Pinkerton agents probably acted as *agents provocateurs*, convincing a few miners to commit isolated acts of violence.

The chief Pinkerton spy was James McParlan, a dashing young Irishman, who, on the orders of Gowen, infiltrated the Hibernians. McParlan was, by all accounts, an engaging fellow, a good barroom companion with a fine Irish tenor and a fine Irish temper. He convinced the Hibernians that he was one of them—that he resented the bosses and wanted a better deal for the miner. He quickly became a leader and instigator of acts of violence. A written account of one confrontation between armed Pinkertons and unarmed miners depicts McParlan leading the miners, "shouting and screaming, two pistols in his belt and a bulldog by his side," and McParlan was allegedly the only "miner" to have a gun.

In another incident publicly blamed on the Mollies, a Gowen-owned coal mine in East Norwegian, Pennsylvania, was destroyed by a fire. Years later, McParlan admitted he had heard that it was set by the owners themselves in order to fan anti-Molly sentiment.

Between 1877 and 1879, nineteen men were convicted

of murder and hanged in connection with the Molly
Maguire conspiracy. The chief witness at all the Molly
trials was James McParlan. All his evidence was either un-
corroborated or had highly questionable corroboration—
that is, by other Pinkerton agents. At the most celebrated
trial, five alleged Mollies were accused of killing a police-
man named Benjamin Yost. The special prosecutor at the
trial was Franklin B. Gowen himself.

The Molly Maguire scare virtually destroyed the union
in Pennsylvania.

Because of the publicity about the Maguires, the state
senate committee which, ironically enough, had been
formed to investigate Gowen's union-breaking activities,
ended up investigating violence in the unions and the
Molly Maguires. After the investigation, it became a crime
even to be a member of a union. In a trial just after the
Molly uproar, a judge passed this sentence: "I find you
Joyce to be President of the Union, and you Maloney to be
Secretary, and therefore I sentence you to one year's im-
prisonment."

In 1880, John Siney died, an embittered, despised, and
disillusioned man with his union in shambles. For over
twenty years after the scandal over the Molly Maguires,
there was not much talk about a union for coal miners in
the anthracite fields of Pennsylvania.

The coal fields of Pennsylvania changed during those
twenty years. New waves of immigrants—Slavs, Hun-
garians, and Italians—began work in the mines. This
mixture of peoples and languages made the prospect of organizing a united front of workers even more difficult. And
although Franklin B. Gowen was dead, his place had been
filled by George F. "Divine Right" Baer, who had earned

his scornful nickname from the following statement of his philosophy:

> The rights and interests of the laboring man will be protected and cared for not by labor agitators, but by Christian men to whom God in his infinite wisdom has given the control of property interests of the country, and upon the successful management of which so much remains.

One can get an idea of the extent of Baer's sympathies and concerns for the laboring man by the response he gave to a reporter's question about the suffering of starving miners: "They don't suffer. They can't even speak English."

However, although the Molly Maguire scare had made things extremely difficult for union organizers in Pennsylvania, the cause of unionism in the mines was far from dead. In other parts of the country, miners' unions grew and became numerous. Many new assemblies were formed under the Knights of Labor. A national convention of the various miners' unions was called in 1890, and they called themselves the United Mine Workers of America.

Although many of the miners' unions had originally been affiliated with the Knights of Labor, they were very practical in outlook, and few looked forward to a revolution. Their first goal was "proper earnings," their second was safety. In their first ten years of existence, they didn't do much to achieve either goal. A large part of the problem was the fact that most of their members were from the mines of the West and the Midwest, while most miners worked in the anthracite fields of Appalachia.

One of the leaders of the new United Mine Workers was

John Mitchell. Like Siney, Mitchell knew mining at first hand. He went to work in the mines at 12 in his native Illinois, and he joined the Knights of Labor when he was 15. He organized the miners in southern Illinois so effectively that at the United Mine Workers convention in 1898 he was elected vice-president at the age of 27, and a year later he was president.

In 1900, Mitchell decided to come East to organize the Pennsylvania anthracite fields. He and his organizers walked into squalid camps and preached the dogma of unionism. He urged the miners to forget their ethnic differences. "The coal you dig isn't Slavish or Polish or Irish coal. It's just coal." He gained the support of many priests and preachers, who became union organizers. One of his most tireless, fearless, and uncompromising organizers was Mother Jones. She had come to America from Ireland in 1835 when she was five years old. She married a member of the Iron Molder's Union and had four children, but a yellow fever epidemic killed her entire family in 1867, and she went back to work. She joined the Knights of Labor in the mid-1870s and in 1880, at the age of 50, she decided to devote her life to the labor movement. She was involved with a number of labor struggles, but the miners and John Mitchell were her special cause. She was 70 in 1900 when John Mitchell asked for her help in organizing the Pennsylvania miners.

Many workers were afraid to strike. In her autobiography Mother Jones describes her experience in Coaldale, Pennsylvania, where the miners were not permitted to assemble in any hall. Mother Jones was driven out of town. She went to a nearby town where the miners were organized, and she asked the miners' wives to help her "free" the miners in Coaldale.

The women fell in behind Mother Jones, bringing their mops and brooms and tin pans. "We marched over the mountains fifteen miles beating on the tin pans as if they were cymbals," wrote Mother Jones.

At three o'clock in the morning, the militia met them on the road to Coaldale and ordered them to go back. Mother Jones and the women would not yield. "Colonel," Mother Jones said, "the working men of America will not halt nor will they ever go back. The working man is going forward!"

The colonel kept them there until daybreak. When he saw it was just an army of women in kitchen aprons, he laughed and let them pass, thinking a group of women wouldn't be able to organize a tough group of miners.

Mother Jones and her women organized all the miners in Coaldale, then did the same in Latimer, a company town where twenty-six union organizers had been murdered in previous strikes. Mother Jones wrote, "The victory of Latimer gave new life to the whole anthracite district. It gave courage to the organization. Those brave women I shall never forget who caused those stone walls to fall by marching around with tin pans and cat calls."

After months of organizing, Mitchell felt strong enough to call a strike in the anthracite fields. The issues were low pay, the lack of a review board to settle wage disputes, poor living conditions in the company towns, and recognition of the union.

The strike was called on September 17, 1900, and settled on October 29. It was a compromise settlement, and in many ways an impressive victory for Mitchell. In a very short time, he had gotten the owners to agree to a ten percent wage increase, as well as a few other concessions, but he received no guarantee of recognition of the miners'

right to organize, and no change in their living conditions.
Mitchell described the strike as

> the most remarkable contest between labor and
> capital in the industrial history of our nations: re-
> markable because it involved a greater number of
> persons than any other industrial contest; because of
> the entire absence of lawlessness on the part of
> those engaged in the strike; and last, but not least,
> because it was the only great contest in which the
> workers came out entirely and absolutely victori-
> ous.

But the 1900 strike settlement had been engineered
largely by powerful Republican businessmen who wanted
a smooth, problem-free election year. Once McKinley was
elected, the Republican leaders lost much of their interest
in John Mitchell's problems.

Between 1900 and 1902, the coal operators frequently
violated the contract. Mother Jones and other brave men
and women who had risked their lives to organize the
union grew restless. They wanted to strike to force the
operators to honor their commitment. Mitchell used all his
influence to prevent a strike. He argued that it was more
important to prove to the public that labor would honor its
side of the bargain—no matter what.

On April 1, 1902, the contract ran out. Mitchell invited
the operators to a joint conference to renegotiate. They
ignored him. Now the very real limitations of the 1900
settlement became apparent. Because Mitchell had settled
for no union recognition at all, the miners were back where
they had started.

Once again, Mitchell called a strike, and Mother Jones

was out in the mining towns talking men into staying away from the mines. The strike began on May 12 and continued throughout the summer and into the fall. It was a hard time for the miners, but the union treasury managed to support them on a bare subsistence level, and they stayed firm.

Many miners became furious with Mitchell because he convinced the miners in other parts of the country not to hold a sympathy strike. The miners in the soft-coal fields of the West and Midwest wanted to show the public that miners stuck together. Mitchell persuaded them to go back to work and honor the existing contract because he felt it would be dishonorable—and poor public relations—to violate it.

Perhaps Mitchell's tactics were right. Public opinion was, for a change, largely on the side of the strikers. Mitchell's often-expressed willingness to compromise impressed the public, and the miners were considerably helped by "Divine Right" Baer's heartless public statements, and his absolute unwillingness to negotiate.

As autumn came with no break in the strike, and with the coal companies' stockpiled reserves running out, there was a general fear that the country would be caught without fuel for the winter.

President Theodore Roosevelt called the leaders of both sides to the White House for a conference. Mitchell agreed to accept the findings of a Presidential commission on the dispute, but Baer absolutely refused, attacking not only the strikers, but also Roosevelt himself for having anything to do with them. "If it wasn't for the high office I hold," Roosevelt told a friend later, "I would have taken him by the seat of the britches and the nape of the neck and chucked him out of the window."

That conference threw even the most conservative public opinion onto the side of the strikers. Moreover, the operators were beginning to feel the pinch. The union was outlasting them, and they were in financial trouble. Of course, the miners themselves were living on bread and water, and no mine operator was near starving. Finally, Roosevelt was so furious he was ready to send the army in to dispossess the owners of the coal mines. The owners finally decided to give in, and told Roosevelt they would accept an arbitration commission, but they made one important stipulation: They would not agree to arbitration if the commission included a representative of labor.

Mother Jones argued with Mitchell to hold out and force the owners to sit down face to face with labor leaders. She told him it was time "to fight to a finish for recognition of the United Mine Workers."

But Mitchell said, "It would never do to refuse the President of the United States."

Mother Jones argued that Mitchell was overawed by the President, too susceptible to flattery from the great Teddy Roosevelt. On March 22, 1903, Mitchell agreed to accept the results of arbitration even if the commission had no representative of labor.

Roosevelt managed to put one labor man on the seven-member commission anyhow, diplomatically describing him as an "eminent sociologist." The commission did come up with a substantial pay raise for the miners—but no guarantee of union recognition.

The result of the 1902 strike was one of the greatest and yet one of the hollowest victories in American labor history. It was a great victory in that the workers won substantial gains, forced a powerful and hard-headed capitalist group to negotiate with them, and gained considerable public acceptance.

But if, after fighting the Revolutionary War and defeating the British armies in the field, George Washington had announced to the American people that from now on the British would give us taxation *with* representation, that would have been an impressive victory of a sort, but not entirely satisfying. So it was with the mine workers. Mitchell accepted so much less than what most labor people thought they could have gotten that the settlement almost seemed like a doublecross.

Nonetheless, Mitchell's victory and hard work in organizing the anthracite fields had turned the Mine Workers Union into the nation's largest union. By 1903, the union had attained a membership of 175,000 and a treasury of a million dollars. When Mitchell resigned in 1908, it had reached 263,000 members.

The United Mine Workers was the first major industry-wide union. It represented all the different crafts working in the mines: miners, sorters, electricians, motormen. A few were highly skilled: some were 11-year-old boys with no skills. However, in 1911, the American Federation of Labor, which was a rather loose collection of unions of different skilled crafts, took in the UMW as an affiliate even though it was not organized by craft. The AFL did not take the mine workers in for idealistic reasons, but simply because they were so strong and numerous.

The mine workers had never been organized by craft because there were simply, as noted before, too many unskilled jobs connected with mining. Furthermore, the miners were too concerned with survival to worry about workers in other industries. At the turn of the century, most miners still worked 12-hour days—often for less than ten dollars a week. Children still worked in the mines. The company owned the towns and charged whatever rents they chose. Most important of all, the owners of the coal companies had never officially been forced to recognize the union's right to exist.

4 : The Rise of John L. Lewis—
The Disastrous Twenties

*Shut down 4,000 coal mines, force 200,000
miners into other industries, and the coal
problem will settle itself.*
John L. Lewis

In 1908, Mitchell was succeeded by Thomas L. Lewis, who was not related to the union's later great president John L. Lewis. Tom Lewis was corrupt and power-hungry, more than willing to feather his own nest at the expense of the workers. He was ousted as president in 1911, the same year the union joined the American Federation of Labor, whereupon Lewis went to work for the owners, selling his knowledge and experience to the other side; he became the Benedict Arnold of the United Mine Workers.

The union's next president was Frank Hayes, a weak, affable man and a heavy drinker. Hayes was succeeded by John L. Lewis in 1920, and Lewis did not step down until 1960, 40 years later. During that time Lewis would become the most important man in American labor, and one of the most important men in American history. For example, in 1937, *The New York Times* devoted approximately one-twentieth of their total news coverage for the year to John L. Lewis. In other words, every day of the year, an average of about two pages of *The New York Times* was devoted to news about Lewis. He received more coverage than the Yankees, Dodgers, and Giants combined, and even more space than that given to President Franklin Delano Roosevelt.

John L. Lewis was born in Lucas, Iowa, on February 12,

1880, the son of a Welsh coal miner. His father, Thomas Lewis, was an organizer for the Knights of Labor, and in 1882, he led a strike against a local mining concern, the White Breast Fuel Company.

This was two years before the great Southwest System Railroad strike established the Knights of Labor as an important force in the American labor movement. Men were afraid to join the union, and organizers like Tom Lewis fought lonely battles, with little hope of support or protection from any quarter.

The miners eventually won their strike against the White Breast Fuel Company, but it was a long and bitter struggle, and by the time it was over its leaders were marked men, especially Tom Lewis. The miners went back to work, but Tom Lewis was blacklisted.

He moved his family to another town, another mine, but the blacklist followed him, and he was soon fired. The Lewises had to move to Des Moines, the state capital, where Tom Lewis got other menial work. Driven out of the coal fields, he was embittered against both the owners whom he had fought and who had blacklisted him, and the men whom he had fought for and who had not supported him. He taught his son John that it wasn't a good thing to trust anybody too much.

John Lewis's formal schooling ended in the eighth grade, and he went to work to help support his family. But due to the influence of his mother and later his wife, Myrta, a schoolteacher, he read widely. He developed a self-taught erudition that made him one of the most extravagantly eloquent orators of his time. "My opponents have smote me hip and thigh," he quoted from Shakespeare at the beginning of one confrontation. "Right merrily shall I return their blows."

In 1897, 15 years after the White Breast Fuel strike, the blacklist on his father was finally lifted, and the Lewises moved back to Lucas, Iowa. John and his younger brother joined his father in the mines. Four years later, when he reached the age of 21, young John L. Lewis restlessly moved west.

He traveled for five years throughout the West, working at a variety of jobs, but always coming back to mining. He mined copper in Montana, silver in Utah, coal in Colorado, and gold in Arizona. In Wyoming, in 1905, he was working for the Union Pacific Coal Company when a monstrous explosion ripped through the mine. Lewis was one of the first to go down into the mine after the explosions, and he helped carry out the 236 bodies of miners killed in the blast.

In 1906, Lewis came back to Lucas, married his child-hood sweetheart, and went back into the mines, where he began to involve himself in the union—so effectively that in the same year he was sent to Indianapolis as the local delegate to the national United Mine Workers convention.

In 1911, when the United Mine Workers joined the AFL, Samuel Gompers, president of the AFL, wanted to do all he could to cement the relationship with his new affiliate. He hired Lewis as a field representative and legislative agent. Lewis spent the next six years traveling for Gompers, from one mining community to another, promoting the cause of the AFL to the miners, and from one state legislature to another lobbying for pro-labor laws.

In the years he worked for Samuel Gompers, Lewis got an education in practical power politics. He learned much from observing Gompers, a shrewd, practical, pragmatic man who knew when to compromise and when to use force—a man who knew, most of all, what worked and how to succeed within practical limitations. Lewis also learned a great deal about political maneuvering from his lobbying activities in the state legislatures and in Congress.

Most important, Lewis was able to use his position and prestige in the AFL to build up his reputation within his own union, the United Mine Workers. He made a lot of friends and allies among UMW officials all over the country during the course of his travels for Gompers, and when, in 1916, he resigned his job with the AFL and accepted a position in the UMW, he had already established the beginnings of his power base.

The position Lewis took with the UMW was that of chief statistician. While the job could have been an undemanding and insignificant one, Lewis was an ambitious man. He took advantage of the job to teach himself a wealth of factual detail about all aspects of the coal mining industry. In later years he came to be respected by unionists and operators alike as the best informed man in the industry. He also corresponded from the UMW home office in Indianapolis with all the local union officials he had met in his travels for the AFL. Since the UMW elected its officers by correspondence, this helped him immeasurably in building up a power base.

Lewis remained chief statistician for only a year. The next year he was voted vice-president. President Frank Hayes became increasingly unable to fulfill his duties because of his drinking problem, and therefore Lewis assumed many of his responsibilities. In 1920, Hayes formally stepped down, and Lewis was elected president.

Lewis began his first term as president of the union with two goals: to bring better wages and working conditions to the men in the coal fields, and to consolidate his power within the union until it was absolute. However he was to concentrate—at least in those early days—on consolidating his power.

In 1920, there was a great deal of unrest among the coal miners of America. They had worked throughout World War I for a wage of five dollars a day, and had agreed, as part of the war effort, not to make any new demands until the war was over. By the autumn of 1919, with the fighting having been ended almost a full year, the UMW convention approved a resolution demanding both a raise in pay and shorter hours. Lewis, of course, was the acting president of that convention, and he was ordered by the gathering to call a strike if the owners did not meet their demands.

President Woodrow Wilson denounced the anticipated strike as illegal, on the grounds that the war was not over yet since he had not yet issued a proclamation of peace. Lewis called the strike anyway, without much enthusiasm. After a month of the strike and much harassment by the federal courts, the press, and the Wilson administration, Lewis met with Wilson at the White House. The next day, much like John Mitchell after his meeting with Theodore Roosevelt, Lewis called off the strike, patriotically announcing, "I will not fight my government, the greatest government on earth." The miners gained nothing.

In retrospect, it seems likely that Lewis was motivated less by patriotism than by two other considerations: his inexperience and his inability to establish his control within the union with a strike in progress.

Once the strike was over, Lewis set about systematically destroying every strong leader who might oppose him in the union. The first to go was Alex Howat, the tough, militant leader of the Kansas miners. Howat was much more willing to call his men out on strike in defiance of court orders than was the cautious Lewis. As a result, he represented a definite threat to Lewis's leadership. Lewis solved the threat by expelling Howat from the union for "unauthorized strikes." Howat took the expulsion very hard, and for many years after that he continued to show up at the United Mine Workers' conventions and demand to be recognized from the floor. When this failed, he would charge down the aisle and try to get up on the podium, and Lewis's bodyguards would pick him up and throw him back down onto the convention floor.

The next target of Lewis's campaign was John Brophy, who was regarded as one of the most honorable and hard-working of union leaders, and one of the most responsive to the needs and feelings of the workers. Brophy and Lewis had deep philosophical differences. In the early 1920s, many within the union believed that the government should nationalize the mines. Lewis had never been comfortable with the idea of socializing the mines. The idea, however, was too popular within his union for him to ignore, and he grudgingly named Brophy head of a three-man study group to come up with a coherent plan for nationalization. Brophy's group put long and careful research into this project and wrote up a detailed proposal wherein the government would buy the mines and run them in such a way as to guarantee maximum employment to a maximum number of workers.

Lewis put the proposal on the shelf. Meanwhile, during the Twenties, miners' wages were slashed again and again. The eight-hour day, a hard-fought union goal from the earliest days of workingmen's organizations, began to yield to nine- and ten-hour days, at no increase in per-day wages. The few mine safety precautions that existed were frequently overlooked by operators, and nothing was done by the union to enforce them.

The Twenties were a period of weakness and disarray in American labor history, and Lewis was not yet a strong leader. On many key issues, he seems to have been downright incompetent. In 1924, in negotiating a new contract for the workers in the bituminous fields, Lewis agreed to a three-year pact with *no* increase in pay. "No backward step!" was his slogan, but the operators broke the contract frequently and cut salaries.

Many mine workers wanted Lewis to push for Brophy's proposal. Nationalization at least would save miner's jobs. Lewis's solution was almost pure laissez-faire capitalism: "Shut down 4,000 coal mines, force 200,000 miners into other industries, and the coal problem will settle itself. It is better to have half a million men working in the industry at good wages . . . than it is to have a million working in the industry in poverty."

Disregarding the fact that Lewis's theory didn't work, and that even the half million who were working did not have good wages, one has to wonder if it is really responsible union leadership to throw half of your membership to the wolves.

On one occasion during this period, when the miners voted overwhelmingly to strike and reject a contract Lewis had negotiated for them, Lewis had the ballots stolen, and then declared that since the ballots were gone he would have to make the decision himself—and his decision was to sign the contract.

Throughout the early Twenties, Brophy fought constantly to get Lewis to be more responsive to the miners' wishes. Finally, in 1926, Brophy decided to run against

Lewis for presidency of the union. He knew it would be a difficult battle since Lewis controlled the union hierarchy almost completely. Brophy realized how Lewis felt about opposition, and he knew if he lost the election he'd be finished in the union. But he decided that if he were to keep faith with his principles at all, he would have to make the try.

His friend Powers Hapgood, a Harvard graduate from a wealthy socialite family who had become a miner and joined the union out of a sense of idealism and dedication to the cause, took Brophy's side and helped him organize his campaign. Unlike Lewis, Brophy was popular and respected, but Lewis had his organization behind him.

An anecdote that was told of how Lewis got votes is probably just a legend, but revealing. A UMW official approaches a worker in the coal fields to show him how to use his ballot. "Now then," he says, "this name on the top line—that's John L. Lewis. You don't like him, do you?"

"No," says the miner. "I hate him."

"Well then," says the UMW man, "we'll just cross him right off the ballot. Put an X next to his name just like this . . ."

But John L. Lewis probably did not use such subtle tactics. He merely stuffed the ballot box with votes for himself, and Brophy lost by a landslide. At the convention the next year, when Powers Hapgood tried to rally support for a protest, he was beaten so badly that he was sent to the hospital.

By the end of the Twenties, Alex Howat, John Brophy, Powers Hapgood, and other reformers like Frank Farrington and George Voyzey, were forced out of the union by various power plays on the part of Lewis. Meanwhile, nearly two-thirds of the rank and file also left, disillusioned by the series of compromises Lewis negotiated with the operators. Many others were forced out of the union because they lost their jobs through automation and mine closings. By the end of the decade, membership in the UMW had shrunk from 450,000 to 60,000, and the remaining members were totally demoralized.

In October 1929, the stock market crashed and America was plunged into the great Depression of the Thirties. But many of the nation's miners couldn't believe any years could be as bad as the Twenties had been.

5 : John L. Lewis and the CIO

*What is it that makes me tick? Is it power
I am after, or am I a Saint Francis in
disguise ...?*
                John L. Lewis

John L. Lewis's presidency of the United Mine Workers had so far been a disaster for everyone in the union except John L. Lewis himself. He seemed like a man determined to use the union as a means of gaining personal power, and along the way it looked like he was going to destroy the union.

In the 1932 election. Lewis supported Herbert Hoover over Franklin D. Roosevelt. In January 1933, when Roosevelt was inaugurated, there were more than 13 million workers unemployed, and about the same number working only part time. There was desperation among the American working classes, and hundreds of thousands of workers demonstrated in the streets for jobs, or for economic relief. Roosevelt had promised the workers some sort of relief and now he had to make good on his promise, because if he did not, there were others who were ready and willing to try. The early Thirties was a time of widespread interest in radical causes and solutions. A Communist-sponsored national demonstration on March 6, 1930, had brought out close to a million people around the country—a hundred thousand each in New York and Detroit alone. Only a very small percentage of those demonstrating workers were actually Communists, or even Communist sympathizers, but they had no qualms about turning out for the demonstration. In the early Thirties, membership in the American Communist party jumped from 8,000 to 24,000. And the moderate wing of the American left also had quite a strong resurgence during the same period. In the 1932 election, the Socialist candidate, Norman Thomas, got close to 900,000 votes.

On June 16, 1933, Roosevelt pushed through Congress his National Recovery Act, a sweeping legislative act designed to put the depression-saddled country back on its feet economically. It was an act designed to regulate the entire structure of American industry. The part of the NRA that was most important to labor was Section 7A, which guaranteed them the right to organize in unions of their own choosing and prohibited employers from refusing a job to anyone for either joining a union or organizing a union. It also made child labor illegal, forced businesses to pay a federal minimum wage, and set up federal regulation of maximum hours. The National Recovery Act meant the end of blacklists and the end of yellow dog contracts.

It was a sweeping, revolutionary law that won for workers far more concessions than their unions had been able to gain for them. Most of Section 7A would be declared unconstitutional in 1935, but by that time some 4 million unemployed had been reabsorbed into industry and about 23 million workers were organized into unions.

But there was a certain irony to the fact that Roosevelt had won for workers the right to organize: most workers had no union to join. Although the AFL had not folded completely, there wasn't much left of it, and its membership represented less than 10 percent of the work force.

The conservative craft-union philosophy of the AFL had become more and more outmoded as mechanization and the assembly line became more and more a part of American industrial life. In 1926, the Ford Motor Company had eight thousand separate job categories. Forty-three percent of them required only one day's training, and another 26 percent needed less than a week. To have eight thousand different craft unions for one industry would clearly be unwieldy. The automobile industry was fast becoming the largest in the United States, and almost all of its workers were unorganized since there was no existing union to take them.

The president of the AFL, William Green, was even more conservative than some business leaders, and could not conceive of organizing labor in anything other than the traditional craft unions. When the president of General Electric told him that if he were going to try and organize GE, he would be better off simplifying matters by organizing them in one industrial union rather than facing the confusion of 15 different craft unions, Green said that he'd take it up with his executive council, then came back and reported to the businessman that such a radical step was out of the question. Either the workers would have craft unions or no unions at all.

If there was going to be a new future in the American labor movement, it became obvious that its direction would not be supplied by William Green.

But no one suspected that a new direction would be supplied by John L. Lewis. Lewis had been every bit as much of a traditional labor conservative as William Green. Not only had he supported Hoover against Roosevelt, but he had squelched every bit of progressive thinking in his own union throughout the Twenties by calling his critics Communists, by physical intimidation, and by ballot-box stuffing.

Yet, Lewis was the first union leader to grasp the importance of Section 7A. He saw that the law provided labor not only with protection, but also with a tremendous psychological boost. For the first time, it seemed that the government was actively encouraging the growth of unions.

In 1933, the United Mine Workers' treasury had only about $75,000 left in it. Lewis gambled all of that money on a nationwide recruiting campaign. Organizers went into every mine, North and South, and their rallying cry was: "The President wants you to join the union!"

His campaign worked phenomenally well. Workers felt that their President, Franklin D. Roosevelt, was on their side and he wanted them to join the union. Inside of a year, the membership of the UMW had soared to over 515,000.

But that was only the beginning for Lewis. He wanted to organize all the unorganized industrial workers in America. It was as if Lewis, now that he was firmly in control of his own union, was finally free to have visions of using his power to actually help the workers. As he put it,

> I had learned the bitter lesson that as long as the great mass of workers was unorganized, so long would it be impossible for organized labor to achieve its legitimate goals. When unions neglect to organize the unorganized, they pay the penalty of their own neglect. I was never permitted to forget that lesson because every year as we sat down to negotiate with the coal operators, they would begin by denying my people a raise in wages and attempt to justify their unreasonable position by citing the lower wage of the steel worker. . . . The low pay of the steel workers was a drag on the wage scale of the United Mine Workers. It became increasingly clear that the mine workers could never really win a just wage until the steel workers were organized and

their miserable wages raised to a just, human standard.

Just as Lewis was the first labor leader to take advantage of the pro-union legislation in 7A and use it for recruiting in his own union, he was the *only* leader to see the full potential of it.

In April of 1933, Lewis talked to Bill Green.

> For two hours, I told him all about the NRA, how it had been engineered and what Section 7A meant. I explained the full potentialities of it to organized labor. Then I asked him to throw the AF of L into a tremendous organizing drive and organize steel, autos, shipbuilding, rubber—everything. Bill argued against it. He said it would cost money, plenty of it. I said, "sure, but it would be worth it." It wasn't a case of really being "worth it"; it was a case of had to, it must be done. I said I would start the ball rolling with half a million dollars. Bill kept hesitating. He talked a bit about how thirty AF of L craft unions hadn't been able to organize in the basic mass production industries.... I emphasized as hard as I could that we must launch industrial organization into these mass industries. Green hesitated and kept saying, "Now, John, let's take it easy."
>
> It was that night...that I knew...that industrial unionization of steel, autos, and the basic industries would never come out of the AF of L.... It was then and there that I knew it was up to me ...I went to bed, and the next day I began to plan the CIO.

Lewis was the vice-president of the AFL at that time. At first his Congress of Industrial Organizations, or CIO, was just a study group within the AFL. True to his nature, Lewis began even his most grandiose schemes slowly. But after his discussion with Bill Green, Lewis knew he had to move out on his own. In 1934, Lewis watched 700,000 workers go out on strike. They were organized on the local level, looking for leadership, but no one was providing it.

An incident in Akron, Ohio, is a good example of how the AFL responded to the new industrial laborers. When five thousand rubber workers applied for an industrial charter, the AFL sent them an organizer who broke them up into 19 different craft unions and refused to accept their charter in any other way.

Craft unionists like Bill Green thought they were protecting themselves with their small but manageable unions. The old-line, conservative labor leaders were simply short-sighted elitists. They felt that the unskilled industrial workers were rabble who could not be counted on to organize themselves effectively, and that they would weaken the bargaining power of the already-existing craft unions if allowed to join. The craft unions were following Lewis's old policy of "Save a few and let the rest go hang."

At the AFL convention of 1935 in Atlantic City, Lewis announced his belief that the AFL should organize unskilled workers. As usual, his booming voice, commanding presence, and incredibly majestic language were enough to make anyone forget that he had ever held any other belief. He told the convention,

> The labor movement is organized upon a principle that the strong shall help the weak. . . . The strength of a strong man is a prideful thing, but the unfortunate thing in life is that strong men do not remain strong. And it is just as true of unions and

labor organizations as it is true of men and individuals.

And whereas today the craft unions of this country may be able to stand upon their own feet and like mighty oaks stand before the gale, defy the lightning, yet the day may come when those organizations will not be able to withstand the lightning and the gale. Now, prepare yourselves by making a contribution to your less fortunate brethren, heed this cry from Macedonia that comes from the hearts of men. Organize the unorganized!

But Lewis's motion was rejected. The convention voted against granting the industrial charter by almost two to one. Big Bill Hutcheson, conservative president of the Carpenter's Union, demanded that all discussion on the subject be stopped.

Lewis walked over to Hutcheson, as he often did during these conventions when there was a problem that had to be ironed out. Hutcheson went halfway to meet him, and the two men stood face to face in the center of the convention floor.

Lewis was a big man, and his commanding presence made him look even bigger. Hutcheson was a huge man, a giant. He weighed close to three hundred pounds.

Lewis spoke quietly. No one ever heard what he said, but Hutcheson's face grew angry as he answered. Those close to them could hear at least one of Hutcheson's words. The word was "bastard."

Then, so quickly that onlookers could scarcely believe they had seen it, Lewis's big coal miner's fist lashed out and staggered Big Bill Hutcheson with a punch to the jaw.

There was a legend that John L. Lewis had once knocked down a man-killing mule named Spanish Pete with his bare hands, and twenty years of working at a desk had not taken all the strength out of his fists. There may have been harder punches thrown in the Thirties—Joe Louis won the heavy-weight championship in that decade—but to the millions of steel workers, auto workers, rubber workers, and workers in all the other unorganized industries in America, that punch made John L. Lewis their heavyweight champion. And it signaled the beginning of a fight that they all could get in on.

It was the fight of the century, and everybody knew it. Its excitement charged the whole labor movement. Powers Hapgood, beaten and driven out of the United Mine Workers by John L. Lewis just a few years before, knew it, and he recalled years later how he "buried the hatchet" and went to work for John L. Lewis. "It was during the 1935 AF of L convention in Atlantic City . . . I watched him, and then I knew I was his man. With Lewis as our leader I knew we were on our way."

Hapgood sent word to Lewis that he wanted to see him. Lewis met him in the lobby of the auditorium and asked him, "Well, Powers, what's on your mind?"

> I said, "I want to come to work for you. I want to help you do what you're talking about. I want to get back into the United Mine Workers. How do I go about it?"
>
> Lewis looked at me and said, "Well, I'll tell you, Powers, there are two ways you can get back into the United Mine Workers Union. One is to get back into the coal pits and start digging coal. Now, I think you have a couple of children, more re-sponsibilities, and you're older. I don't think that would be such a good way. The second course would be to accept a position working for the United Mine

Workers of America, and I want you to come with us. We're about to go off into a campaign that... will be everything you've dreamed about and everything you've talked about. We're going out to fight for those things, and we're going to get them. You see, Powers, I've never really opposed those things. I just never felt that the time was ripe and that trying to do those things back in the days when we had our violent arguments would have been suicide for organized labor and would have resulted in complete failure. But now, the time is ripe, and now the time to do those things is here. Let us do them."

Lewis stopped talking, and I can't tell you how I felt. It was just as though everything I dreamed of had finally come to pass.

Was Lewis telling his old enemy the truth? Had he truly been planning this all along, all the while that he was chasing Hapgood, Brophy, and others out of the union for advocating these very causes? Had he just been waiting for the right moment? As he himself once asked, impishly: "What is it that makes me tick? Is it power I am after, or am I a Saint Francis in disguise, or what?"

"I am for labor," Lewis announced. "And I will go with anyone who will work with me in this cause." Almost everyone went with him. Brophy came back too, as Lewis's choice for executive director of the new CIO. Communists and socialists joined the cause, and Lewis didn't chase them away. They hoped that a strong, organized working class might eventually be able to take the means of production into their own hands and do away with the capitalist system altogether. Intellectuals took up the cause of labor as well. Clifford Odets wrote a play, *Waiting for Lefty*, produced in 1935, which ended with the entire audience joining the actors on stage in an emotion-filled chant of "Strike! Strike!"

Most of all, there were the workers. With Lewis's skilled organizers to coordinate them, or acting on their own, the workers in the rubber industry, in the electrical-appliance industry, the newspaper industry, shipbuilding, glass, oil, transportation, and many others organized as industrial unions.

The steel industry was one of the biggest, and the toughest to organize. Finally, in 1937, the big steel companies recognized the steel workers' union, headed by Lewis's closest associate from the United Mine Workers, Philip Murray. It was a tremendous victory for Lewis and the CIO.

But the auto industry was where the hardest struggle was fought, and the greatest victory was won. In 1937, General Motors, the nation's largest corporation, was hit by a sit-down strike. The workers not only went on strike, but also refused to leave the factory, making it impossible for GM to bring in strikebreakers.

General Motors denounced the tactic as illegal. It was more radical than Lewis himself might have wished, but he placed the CIO's support squarely behind the strikers. His days of leaving his striking members in the lurch seemed to be over. General Motors was finally forced to give in and negotiate with the striking workers. The owners recognized the right of their workers to organize as an industry.

Thus, by 1937, with the organization of practically all the major American industries, the CIO was clearly established as the most important force in American labor, and there was even talk of John L. Lewis becoming Roosevelt's next vice president.

6 : John L. Lewis and the United Mine Workers in World War II

Speaking for the American Soldier, John
Lewis, damn your coal black soul.
Stars and Stripes, 1943

Certainly the two most popular figures in America to the working classes at the end of the Thirties were John L. Lewis and Franklin D. Roosevelt. In thousands of miners' cabins, their two pictures could be found side by side above the mantelpiece.

And there was no question that Lewis was politically ambitious. It was reliably reported that Lewis told Roosevelt he wanted to be his running mate. Supposedly their conversation went like this:

> Lewis: "Mr. President, a ticket that incorporated the two most prominent men in America would be invincible."
> Roosevelt: "Yes, John, and which place will you take?"

Almost all historians agree that Roosevelt had no intention of making John L. Lewis his vice-president, however much he might have dangled that bait before Lewis. The two men were too much alike—and one of the ways that they were most alike was that neither man could stand the idea of sharing the limelight with another strong man.

As a result, tension developed between the two. On Memorial Day, 1937, the police in Chicago killed ten steelworkers during a demonstration outside the gates of the Republic Steel Corporation. Roosevelt, asked to com-

ment on the affair, quoted Shakespeare: "A plague o' both
your houses!" He was exasperated with the constant labor-
management struggle that was draining his efforts to restore
the economy.

Lewis was furious that Roosevelt had not been sympathetic to the plight of the dead steelworkers. In a radio
speech that Labor Day, Lewis blasted Roosevelt with one of
his most stinging and flamboyant oratorical flights:

> Labor, like Israel, has many sorrows. Its women
> weep their fallen and they lament for the children
> of the race. It ill behooves one who has supped at
> Labor's table to curse with equal fervor and fine
> impartiality both labor and its adversaries when they
> become locked in deadly embrace.

Lewis had supported Roosevelt in the election of 1936,
and Roosevelt owed much of his great victory to labor's
effort. By 1940, however, there was no more talk of Lewis
as FDR's next possible running mate. The feud between
the two was well known, and yet everyone expected Lewis
to at least nominally support Roosevelt.

But once again Lewis confounded his followers. He
gambled his entire prestige, his career as leader of the
American labor movement, on defeating Roosevelt. He
personally campaigned for Wendell Wilkie, Roosevelt's
opponent. On a nationwide radio broadcast in October
1940, he announced:

> It is obvious that President Roosevelt will not be re-
> elected unless he has the overwhelming support of
> the men and women of labor. If he is, therefore,
> re-elected, it will mean that the members of the
> Congress of Industrial Organizations have rejected
> my advice and recommendation. I will accept the

result as being the equivalent of a vote of no con-
fidence, and will retire as President of the Congress
of Industrial Organizations in November.

Lewis was asking the working men and women of
America to choose between him and their president. He
wanted to be the only picture on the mantelpiece. However, in 1940 the world was clearly at the edge of war, and
no one wanted to go into the uncertain years ahead without the one man they trusted, Franklin D. Roosevelt. The
working men and women overwhelmingly ignored Lewis
and chose Roosevelt.

Lewis kept his promise. He resigned as president of the
CIO and nominated Phillip Murray, a man who had been
with Lewis from the early days of the United Mine Workers Union. Murray had a burning desire to show that he
was not just a pawn of John L. Lewis.

The CIO became split over the issue of international
politics. Lewis believed that the United States should stay
out of Europe's politics. One of the major reasons for his
break with Roosevelt was that he believed Roosevelt would
lead the country to war.

On June 22, 1940, Hitler's Nazi armies invaded the
Soviet Union. Lewis discovered that a large number of the
union leaders who supported him suddenly left his side,
and began to attack him publicly for his isolationist stand.
Finally in 1942, the United Mine Workers Convention
voted 2867 to 5 to leave the organization that was attacking
their leader. The rest of Lewis's active life was to be carried
out where he had started, in the United Mine Workers.

Many of the battles of the 1940s had to do with enforcing a provision Lewis had won for the miners in 1939.
This was the "union security" clause, which meant that
the coal operators agreed to the end of the open shop, a

shop which employs both union and nonunion labor. The new contract guaranteed a union shop, a closed shop in which the mine operators agreed to hire only card-carrying, dues-paying UMW members.

The union argument for the closed shop is two-fold. First, in an open shop, subtle and not-so-subtle pressures can be put on workers not to join the union. Second, since all workers are paid the same, why should a worker who does not pay dues to support the union get the same benefits as a dues-paying union worker?

Today the combination of the union shop and restrictive membership rules in many trade unions has created a new form of tyranny against many American workers. The union can refuse to admit more than a few new members, and nonmembers can't find work in union-controlled trades or industries. Racism and sexism are all too common in American labor, and the closed shop is often a means of closing opportunities to blacks and women. However, in 1939, after decades of ruthless exploitation of the worker who belonged to a union, the closed shop seemed like an unquestioned blessing.

The next few years, of course, were the war years. All of American labor turned its efforts to supporting the national war effort. With so many of the young men off at war, women took over in the factories doing skilled, heavy labor. They were welders, riveters, and carpenters, doing all the jobs that many men today assume women can't possibly handle. Whole industries turned their means of production over to the war effort. Instead of automobiles, they built jeeps and tanks. Instead of clothing, they made parachutes, army blankets, weapons, and electronic devices for radar. Within months, entire lines of products changed and industries got fat, profitable government contracts for their goods. Organized labor turned its fate over to the National War Labor Board, with representatives from labor, management, and the public. This board would set wages and benefits, and the workers pledged not to strike for the duration of the war.

John L. Lewis initially supported this policy. His miners had been out on strike on Pearl Harbor Day. "When the nation is attacked," said Lewis, "every American must rally to its defense. All other considerations become insignificant." The strike was settled that day.

Lewis maintained this attitude for two years. Then, in the heart of the war, the middle of 1943, Lewis called his miners out on strike. Coal, in a slump since the Twenties, was booming as an important war industry, and Lewis wanted more for the miners.

Lewis was not blindly sabotaging the war effort. He knew more about every facet of the coal industry than any other man in America, and every time he struck during the war, he knew that the coal companies had enough of a stockpile so that the flow of coal to fuel the war machine was never in danger of being interrupted.

Nevertheless, by calling a strike during wartime, Lewis became the most hated man in America. But he felt that the time to win more for the miners was while the coal companies were sitting fat and pretty. He first called the miners out on May 1, 1943. Roosevelt made a strenuous appeal to suspend the strike at least until the War Board could rule on the union's demand. Lewis sent the miners back to work.

Dissatisfied with the War Labor Board's ruling, the miners struck again on May 25. This time, an enraged Congress quickly enacted the Smith-Connally Act, which made it a crime to strike during wartime.

The New York Times described the law as "hasty, ill-considered and confused." Philip Murray, the new president of the CIO, called it "the most vicious attack on labor and labor's rights in the history of the nation." Roosevelt, angry as he was with Lewis, vetoed the bill, but Congress in turn overrode the veto.

The miners went back to work on June 7th, pending another War Labor Board ruling. When the ruling came, on June 18th, they struck again.

The overseas Army newspaper, *Stars and Stripes*, published a cartoon showing John L. Lewis, with his eyebrows and miner's hat, throwing dirt on the grave of an American soldier, and an editorial concluded with the words: "Speaking for the American soldier, John Lewis, damn your coal black soul."

The fact is that despite the tidal wave of criticism and revulsion against Lewis and the miners, there was no stoppage of the flow of coal. The amount of work time that was lost by strikes during World War II, in all of organized labor—including the coal industry—was less than one-tenth of one percent of the total available working time.

And, of course, there was one group of Americans who did not hate John L. Lewis: the mine workers. After the wartime strikes of 1943, a long and bitter strike in 1946, and a shorter one in 1949, they were the best-paid group of workers in America.

7. Corruption and the Welfare and Retirement Fund

Provision should be made in all union
contracts for the recall of leaders.
—Mother Jones

In the late Forties, it seemed to most miners that John L. Lewis could do no wrong. One of his greatest accomplishments was the establishment of the first pension fund, considered by many the greatest single benefit ever won for American workers.

Beginning with the strike of 1946, Lewis got the government agency which controlled the mines at that time, in a special post-wartime procedure, to agree that the mine owners should pay a royalty of five cents on every ton of coal mined in America in order to establish a miners' welfare and retirement fund.

The fund was a separate organization from the union. It was directed by three trustees—Lewis, representing the union, a representative of the coal companies, and a neutral third party. The neutral third party was Josephine Roche, once a small mine owner herself, but for years a close friend of Lewis's. During the entire time they were co-trustees of the fund, she never voted against Lewis on any issue.

The first payments made through the fund came the following year, 1947. A grim accident made it horribly clear why the fund was needed: A mine exploded in Centralia, Illinois, and killed 111 miners. Their families were paid $1,000 each in death benefits by the fund. Although the amount of compensation was small, it was the first time in the whole death-filled history of American coal mining that any financial relief was given to the family of a striken miner, and a great improvement from the times when the widows and orphans of mine-disaster victims were evicted from their company-owned homes.

After the coal strike of 1949, the royalties were increased to 20¢ a ton, and part of the money was set aside to give a retirement pension of $100 a month to miners over 60 years old who had worked in the mines for more than 20 years. In 1949, Horace Ainscough got the first pension check ever issued, and blessed the day that John L. Lewis was born.

In 1951, construction was started on ten hospitals in Kentucky, West Virginia, and the western part of Virginia. The Mine Workers Welfare and Retirement Fund put $30 million into the project, and when the hospitals were opened in 1956, they brought modern, quality medical services to the area for the first time.

The hospitals were owned by nonprofit corporations funded almost entirely by the Welfare and Retirement Fund. Although the hospitals were operated for the miners their facilities were available to everybody.

Yet, despite their high pay and new pension fund, the coal miners faced many problems in the Fifties. After the war boom and the first peacetime push back to the production of consumer goods, the coal industry went into a slump. Other forms of power, such as natural gas and electric power, had become cheaper to produce; coal production fell off, resulting in fewer jobs for miners. At the same time, new mechanized mining techniques meant even fewer jobs.

John L. Lewis's reaction was strange. He seemed more concerned with the plight of the owners of the coal mines than with that of his workers. He claimed that in helping the coal industry, he was in the long run helping his miners.

He argued that it was a good opportunity for young men to get out of mining and go into healthier occupations. He did nothing to safeguard jobs and nothing to make life easier for the miners who had lost their jobs. Pensions were for miners who had worked continuously for years. There was no benefit for the miner who had, for example, worked for five years and then been laid off; all the money he had put into the union as dues was lost to him.

In 1949, the union bought a controlling interest in the National Bank of Washington, and Lewis transferred $36 million of Welfare and Retirement Fund money into a checking account that was not earning interest for the Welfare Fund.

It was John L. Lewis's idea to buy the bank, and his idea to put the $36 million into a checking account. In order to do it, he needed the approval of the trustees of the fund. The trustee who represented the coal company, Charles L. Owen, voted against the transfer. He protested that the money should at least be invested in a savings account so that it would earn interest for the miners. But he was voted down by Lewis and his good friend Josephine Roche, and the transfer went through.

Why did Lewis want the union to own a bank, and why did he want $36 million in a checking account? He used the money to benefit the coal companies instead of the miners.

Lewis is a very strange man, and a very strange study in the desire for power. In the 1920s he had seized power in the union, and neglected the miners in order to consolidate his hold on the union. In the 1930s he rose to national power by risking all on the CIO. In the 1940s he risked his power on defeating FDR, and he was thrown back to the

fiefdom of his own union. For nearly a decade, he worked to
bring benefits to his union, but then perhaps he became
bored with being the most powerful man in the union, and
he wanted to become the most powerful man in the entire
coal industry. The best way to accomplish this goal was to
show the operators that he could do more for them than
anyone else could. It was generally agreed that no one
knew more about the coal industry than John L. Lewis,
and now John L. Lewis had the money to make the best of
his knowledge. He loaned millions of dollars to mine owners who were having trouble in the 1950s. He made an
incredible round of secret deals with coal companies and
with other corporations that made heavy use of coal.
Clearly, Lewis was using the union's money in a most
unethical way.

And he used the union's power in some very unsavory
ways, too. In Kentucky and Tennessee, for example, there
were a number of nonunion mines. The union set out to
organize them, but in many cases, the workers did not
want to be organized. The owners of the big mines wanted
those mines organized so that small mines would have to
pay union wages and the now 40¢-per-ton royalty to
the fund. In each new contract, Lewis had upped the
amount per ton, and the mine operators had agreed to the
new price. With these added expenses, the small mines
would not be able to undersell the big mines. In this regard,
John L. Lewis had grown to think of himself as the partner
to the big operators.

He ordered the small mines to be organized. His union
men came in and began employing the tactics that the
Baldwin-Felts detectives of the Twenties and Thirties had
used to stop the union. They dynamited equipment,

threatened workers, blocked the entrances and exits to mines, and threatened the lives of the truckers who carried the coal.

And in one instance, the union was charged with trying to order a murder. In 1952, Charles Minton sued the union for firing him from his job because he refused to commit a murder. Minton testified that he had been blowing up the property of the Gladeville Coal Company in southern Virginia, on orders from the union. Then he got a new order from a man who introduced himself as a "personal agent of John L. Lewis." The order was to kill the two owners of the Gladeville Coal Company.

Minton, who had no scruples about dynamiting property, balked. He refused to kill, and the union fired him, and saw to it that he was blacklisted from the mines.

The lawsuit was settled out of court and forgotten. In 1970, when reporters went back to check the story, the court records had mysteriously disappeared. All that was left was a few people's memories, and the back file of the local newspaper, which carried the full story of the filing of the lawsuit, including the name of the "personal agent of John L. Lewis," Tony Boyle, who was later to succeed Lewis as leader of the UMW.

Eventually, most of the small mines were either organized or went bankrupt—sometimes the former causing the latter.

Meanwhile, the Welfare and Retirement Fund, which was providing the capital to keep the coal companies in business, was doing less and less well by its members. Lewis began changing the rules so that he would have to pay less money to the miners, and thus have more for his many deals.

The first change in the rules came in 1953, just four years

after the fund was formed. The original by-laws had said
that any miner who had worked for 20 years in the mines
could get a pension. But this was modified to read that
those 20 years had to have been compiled within the 30
years previous to the application for the pension. Therefore,
any miner who had worked in the mines more than thirty
years ago found that he did not qualify for benefits.

Naturally, the first people hurt by the change were the
old-timers. If a miner had worked from 1922 to 1942, and
then applied for a pension in 1953 upon reaching the age
of 62, he was not eligible, because only 19 of his years in
the mines had been since 1923. He was ineligible for any
money at all.

For a time, other, younger miners continued to support
John L. Lewis and their union, not realizing they would
be affected by his policies too. One West Virginia miner
worked for 28 years in the mines, starting when he was
15. He was a loyal supporter of the union, a vice-president
of his local for four years. In 1949, he was crippled in a
mine accident. He couldn't work any more, so he waited
until 1965, when he reached the right age to apply for his
pension. It was only then that he discovered that the years
he had worked before 1935 didn't count. He was not entitled to any pension at all.

In 1954, all cash benefits to disabled miners and widows
and children of dead miners were stopped abruptly, because only pensions and medical care were specifically
covered in the fund's regulations. The aid for widows and
disabled had been "temporary," Lewis said, and only a
means of promoting the fund when it was getting started.
But 55,000 people who had nowhere else to turn, and who
had never been given any warning that the aid was temporary, were suddenly cut off.

The most shocking changes of all were made in the early Sixties. The first of these, in 1960, changed the regulations for hospital and medical care to exclude miners who had been out of work for more than a year. This change came at a time when, because of the recession and spreading automation, large numbers of miners *had* been out of work for more than a year. The provisions also stated that any miner who was currently working in a nonunion mine was also not able to receive benefits, even if he had previously worked in a union mine, while a worker who had worked all his career in a nonunion mine, and had only recently joined the union would be entitled to full benefits.

Then, later in 1960, while the fund was being used to make multimillion-dollar loans to multimillionaire coal owners, the miners' pensions were cut from $100 a month to $75 a month. The miners could do nothing. Their representative as trustee of the fund was their union president, John L. Lewis, and it was he who had initiated the cut.

In 1962, the fund cut off all benefits to miners working in mines that had not kept up their royalty payments. This was unfair because it penalized the miners for the shortcomings of the mine owners, and also because in many cases, the owners had been secretly encouraged by the union not to pay their royalties.

Lewis was concerned that the royalty payments would create such a burden on the coal operators that they would shut the mines down.

As another money-saving move, the fund decided in the same year that the union hospitals were to be shut down. The hospitals were saved at the last minute by the Presbyterian Church, which bought them from the fund with the help of a six-million-dollar grant from the Federal govern-

ment, pushed through by a direct order from President
Kennedy.

Mother Jones, in her autobiography written in 1925
when she was 95, long before Section 7A, before the CIO,
the war strikes, and the fund, described and foreshadowed
the history of the UMW:

> As I look back over the long, long years, I see that
> in all movements for the bettering of men's lives, it
> is the pioneers who bear most of the suffering.
> When these movements become established, when
> they become popular, others reap the benefits. Thus
> it has been with the labor movement. . . .
>
> Many of our modern leaders of labor have wan-
> dered far from the thorny path of these early cru-
> saders. Never in the early days of the labor struggle
> would you find leaders wining and dining with the
> aristrocracy, nor did their wives strut about like
> diamond-bedecked peacocks; nor were they at-
> tended by humiliated, cringing colored servants.
>
> The wives of those early leaders took in washing
> to make ends meet. Their children picked and sold
> berries. The women shared the heroism, the priva-
> tion of their husbands.
>
> In those days labor's representatives did not sit on
> velvet chairs in conference with labor's oppressors;
> they did not dine in fashionable hotels with the
> representatives of the top capitalists. . . . They did
> not ride in Pullmans or make trips to Europe.
>
> The rank and file have let their servants become
> their masters and dictators. The workers have got to
> fight not alone their exploiters, but likewise their
> own leaders, who often betray them, who sell them
> out, who put their own advancement ahead of that

of the working masses, who make of the rank and file political pawns.

Provisions should be made in all union contracts for the recall of leaders. Big salaries should not be paid. Career hunters should be driven out as well as leaders who use labor for political ends. These types are menaces to the advancement of labor.

In big strikes I have known, the men lay in prison while the leaders got out on bail and drew high salaries all the time. The leaders did not suffer. They never missed a meal.

8: Tony Boyle and the Selling out of the Miners

We follow the judgment of the coal operators, right or wrong.
Tony Boyle

John L. Lewis didn't retire as president of the United Mine Workers until 1960, when he was 80 years old. For decades no one had ever opposed him in an election, despite all his machinations with the fund. When he retired, he was honored by a testimonial banquet that was attended by representatives of the coal companies as well as by union officials. He was honored by all as a "labor statesman," and he kept his role as one of the three trustees of the retirement fund.

His place as union president was taken by Thomas Kennedy, a long-time associate of Lewis who had been vice-president of the union for almost twenty years. At 72, Kennedy was almost as old as Lewis, and his health was failing. It was obvious to everyone, including Lewis, that Kennedy would not be president for long. The really important office to be filled was Kennedy's former position as vice-president of the union. Lewis picked Tony Boyle, who was accepted by all as Lewis's chosen heir.

Boyle had been an administrative assistant to Lewis in the Washington headquarters of the UMW for 12 years. There were other able men who worked in the field as organizers who might have been picked. Joseph "Jock" Yablonski, for example, president of the union's District 5 in Pennsylvania, had often been singled out for praise by Lewis. "He's my right-hand man," old John L. had said of him publicly. "Whenever I have trouble in the coal fields, I need him." Privately, Lewis had hinted to Yablonski more than once that he might be president of the union someday. Yablonski was a strong, forceful man with a popular appeal to many miners. He had worked among them, and many knew him personally.

But when it came time to choose his heir, Lewis chose a man from headquarters. Perhaps Lewis really felt that Boyle had the best qualifications. Perhaps a knowledge of the bureaucratic power structure of headquarters was a more important qualification for union leadership than an intimate, first-hand knowledge of mines and miners.

On the other hand, Boyle was not totally unqualified for the job. He had been born in 1901 in a cabin in a little Montana mining town, the son of an immigrant miner, and the grandson of a miner. He quit school to go into the mines. Then, much like the young John L. Lewis, he wandered around the West, sometimes working in the mines, sometimes aboveground. He came back to Montana and worked his way up in the union hierarchy, becoming vice-president of the Montana CIO in 1938. In 1948, he came to work for Lewis in Washington.

Nobody knows exactly what Tony Boyle did in Washington. His title was always administrative assistant. The closest thing there is to a clear record of one of his activities is Charles Minton's claim that Boyle tried to hire him for an assassination, and Boyle of course denied that.

Boyle's tenure as administrative assistant to Lewis stretched through the years when Lewis was most powerful, most secretive, most concerned with the industry, and least responsive to the miners. And what Tony Boyle learned about power was that it was centered in the union headquarters in Washington, and that it could be used to get almost anything. Boyle used this power in the most obvious way, by cheating the dues-paying miners and obtaining blatantly unethical or illegal favors for his family.

Tony's brother Jack became a mine operator in 1954, forming a company called the Mountain States Mining Company. A few years earlier, Boyle's other brother, Dick, had become president of Tony's old District 27 in Montana, despite the fact that Dick had never been a miner, and union regulations required an officer to have at least five years' experience in the mines. When Jack got his mine, Dick suddenly became concerned with mine safety, and pressured the area's Federal mine inspectors into closing down most of Jack's nearby competitors for safety reasons. At the same time, other competitors were suddenly hit by a rash of UMW-ordered strikes.

Dick Boyle seemed to think that closing down his brother's competitors was all that needed to be done about mine safety. The Montana legislature, however, began to hold hearings in 1957 on some proposed mine-safety laws. One law would have required roof bolts in all the mines— one of the most basic of all modern safety precautions, and one of the most needed, since roof cave-ins are the most common mine accident. Tony Boyle flew to Montana to give his expert testimony—*against* the bill. He argued, incomprehensibly, that the law would "legalize the killing of men in coal mines." He argued that the largest coal mine in the state (which happened to belong to his brother Jack) would have to shut down if it were forced to install roof bolts in all its roofs. The bill was defeated. And then, on January 28, 1958, the roof of Boyle's brother's mine collapsed, killing four men.

Here is a list of some of Tony Boyle's expenditures out of union dues:

• His brother Dick Boyle received a $25,000 salary as president of District 27, a job that had little responsibility since by the Sixties there was very little mining done in District 27 and very few union members. He also got $17,000 in 1967 for "organizing expenses," even though no organizing was done.

• Tony's daughter Antoinette was hired as District 27 staff counsel. The district was small enough that it barely required a part-time lawyer, but Tony's daughter received $40,000 a year—eight times the amount of the total union dues collected in the state of Montana, the district she was representing. Her salary equaled that of the lawyer who handled the legal problems for the entire union.

• Boyle set up his own pension fund for "Resident International Officers"—that is, himself, Secretary-Treasurer John Owens, and retired President Lewis. Boyle and Owens transferred $650,000 into this special pension fund without telling anyone, and then took advantage of the confused way that UMW records were kept to ensure that no one found out.

Another of Boyle's favorite ways of wasting union funds was publicity photos. Between 1963 and 1969, the American coal miners paid $200,000 for portrait photographs of union officials—the vast majority of them of Tony Boyle.

The rank and file did get to see the results of this particular expenditure. The UMW Journal, formerly a respected labor periodical that brought the miners a good complete news source about mines, mining, and the union, became completely a publicity organ for Tony Boyle. Boyle's pictures were spread throughout every issue, along with article after article about him, and all the things he was doing to benefit the union members.

When Boyle negotiated a new UMW contract in 1968, the Journal celebrated it with a picture of Boyle on the front cover, six pictures of Boyle on the back cover, and five more pictures of Boyle scattered throughout the 24 pages of the issue. The lead article was headlined THE BOYLE WAGE CONTRACT, and went on to describe the "President Boyle National Bituminous Coal Wage Agreement of 1968," which was probably the first union contract ever to be named.

Tony Boyle actually became president of the union in early 1963, when Thomas Kennedy died, although Kennedy's illness had left the union essentially in Boyle's hands since 1960.

In the years from 1960 to 1963, Boyle had begun to see more and more clearly that this business of being czar of all the miners was not going to be as simple as he had first thought. He was not automatically going to inherit the reverence that the miners had felt for John L. Lewis. No matter how autocratic Lewis had been, the miners had trusted him, and that kind of feeling has to be earned. Perhaps Boyle never realized this, or couldn't accept it.

For another thing, while Boyle might nominally be in power, John L. Lewis, even in his eighties, was still very much a part of the picture. Lewis still had his office on the sixth floor of the UMW building, and his presence still loomed large. The strongest men in America, including Franklin D. Roosevelt, had found it hard to stand up to Lewis, and Tony Boyle was no exception.

By January 1963, when Tom Kennedy died and Boyle took over as president, the economy had recovered from a temporary recession, and the miners felt they were in a position to push for new demands. They wanted safety regulations and job protection strengthened, an end to the massive layoffs caused by mechanization, and a new seniority clause. The miners wanted other minor but important benefits too, such as bathhouses so they could wash up after work.

The old union contract had been open-ended: that is, there was no set date for it to expire. When Boyle took over the presidency, the miners expected him to open talks for a new contract right away. But although Tony talked tough and seemed to know what the men wanted, the year dragged on, and there were no contract talks. The miners began to get very impatient, and many of them were on the verge of a strike—a strike against the union, to get them to reopen the contract.

Finally, contract talks were opened on December 18, 1963. Everyone thought Boyle was going to fight hard for what the miners wanted. But when the new agreement was signed in March 1964, it gave the miners a two-dollar a day wage boost and none of the benefits the miners really wanted.

Around ten thousand men walked out in protest, "wild-cat" strikes, that is, strikes called without union authorization. The strike against "two-dollar Tony" and his contract lasted about a week, and then the miners went back to work.

One important issue to the miners was autonomy, the right to elect their own district officials, a right that had been taken away from the local district members. In all but 5 of the 27 districts, the officers were appointed by headquarters in Washington. Lewis had been too greatly loved and feared for anyone to protest, but now under Boyle many miners were very dissatisfied with their lack of freedom.

A new law, the Landrum-Griffin Act passed in 1959, made the practice of appointing district officials illegal. It was this law also that forced the UMW to disclose its financial holdings, so that the miners and the public learned about the National Bank of Washington and its holdings, and the multimillion-dollar loans to coal operators. Despite the law's provisions that all district officers be elected, however, five years after its passage nothing had changed in the UMW districts.

In 1964, Tony Boyle had to campaign for his first official, elected term as president of the union. Before the beginning of a campaign, the union traditionally held its convention. Theoretically, the purpose of a UMW convention was to vote on resolutions submitted by union locals, having to do with union policy and objectives. But Boyle wanted the 1964 convention to be a giant outpouring of overwhelming support for him that would spill over to the election. Boyle knew there were likely to be challenges to his leadership at the convention, and he was determined to squelch them.

His first move was to hold the convention in Bal Harbour, Florida, far away from the coal fields of Pennsylvania, Illinois, or West Virginia, making it difficult and expensive for many miners to get there. To make it even more difficult and more expensive, he extended the convention from a week to 11 days.

His next step was to make sure that those delegates who *did* support him were able to afford to attend. Boyle arranged 500 convention jobs, from ushers and messengers to sergeants-at arms. Each job paid $60 a day, and they all went to friendly delegates. In all, more than 500 out of the 1,173 delegates were being paid by Boyle to be there. And to make sure that all his friends had a good time, Boyle brought in four bands. In total, the pro-Boyle demonstrations cost the union over $300,000.

For his critics, there was another kind of reception. Led

by tough, ruthless secretary-treasurer Albert Pass, District 19 supplied unofficial marshals to the convention—a battalion of burly miners in white hard hats that had "District 19" written on one side and "Tony Boyle" on the other. District 19 covered southeastern Kentucky and eastern Tennessee. It was the district that had supplied the union gun thugs of the Fifties, and it had a fearsome reputation. On the first day of the convention, when an anti-Boyle delegate rose to question the seating arrangements on the convention floor, he was brutally beaten into submission by the District 19 thugs.

Jock Yablonski, furious, sought out Boyle and told him that if the rough stuff continued, he would lead his District 5 delegation out of the convention. Boyle promised it would not be repeated, but the white hard hats stayed next to all the microphones, and their point had been made.

The result of the convention was a complete victory for Boyle and his group. Autonomy was voted down because the delegates said the miners didn't want it. There were 279 motions asking for reforms in the welfare fund, and they were all voted down. The president's term in office was extended from 4 years to 5, and the number of endorsements by locals needed to nominate a presidential candidate was raised from 5 to 50.

This last move was basically intended to prevent anyone from running against Boyle for the presidency. A Pennsylvania miner, Steve "Cadillac" Kochis, was gearing up to run against him in the 1964 election to be held that December, but Kochis had no money and no publicity, and eventually lost by more than five to one. Boyle, however, hated the idea that he was not the unanimous choice of all the miners, and so he squelched the chance for opposition. In the future, with the tightly controlled dictatorship of the United Mine Workers, and with the issue of autonomy shelved, it would be almost impossible for anyone to get the endorsement of 50 locals.

In spite of Boyle's successfully controlled convention and election, peace and harmony did not automatically return to the coal fields. Wildcat strikes erupted here and there during the following year. In West Virginia, six miners, five of them UMW officials, were fired after protesting to a coal company about safety conditions. The men who worked with them went out on strike in sympathy. Soon the strike spread throughout Ohio, northern West Virginia, and southwestern Pennsylvania, and closed down 15 percent of the nation's coal production for almost a month. The strike was finally ended when Tony Boyle promised he would do everything he could to get the men reinstated, but it was a hollow promise.

Nevertheless, the coal industry was in a boom period. The miners had work, and they were relatively happy. The 1968 UMW convention—again held far away from the coal fields, in Denver, Colorado—was uneventful, except for a couple of resolutions calling for the installation of Tony Boyle as president for life, and the doubling of Tony Boyle's salary to $100,000. These resolutions were probably conceived of by Boyle or his staff, to make him look good when he turned them down, which he did. Lifetime presidency or not, it looked as though Tony Boyle would be in power as long as he wanted, just like John L. Lewis before him.

9 : The Clean-up Campaign

Coal miners don't have to die.
Congressman Ken Hechler

On the morning of November 20, 1968, the number nine mine of the Consolidation Coal Company, one of the biggest coal producers in Appalachia, was rocked with a tremendous explosion, and 78 men were trapped underground. For nine days the fires raged through the mines, as rescuers tried to find some way to get through to the trapped victims, but they finally gave up when they decided there was no way that the men could still be alive.

Tony Boyle, representing the UMW, arrived at Farmington 56 hours after the explosion. He wore a suit and sported a rose in his lapel. The rose was his trademark. He complained irritably about having to talk to the families of the victims, and in his statement to the press concerning the explosion he commented rather callously that "as long as we mine coal, there is always this inherent danger."

The Farmington mine had failed 16 inspections for safety precautions to prevent coal dust explosions in the past five years. However, with 78 coal miners trapped in the raging inferno underground, and with their grief-stricken families standing in his audience, Tony Boyle praised the Consolidation Coal Company as "one of the best companies to work with as far as health and safety are concerned," and flew back to Washington.

It wasn't the rose in his lapel, or his not talking to the miners' families that made Farmington the beginning of the end for Tony Boyle. It wasn't even his unsolicited, on-the-spot testimonial for the coal company. What happened after Farmington was that people outside the union began to notice what was happening to the miners.

There were people who should have noticed before. The Justice Department, under Attorney-General Robert Kennedy, had rooted out corruption in the Teamsters Union. Kennedy had proved that Jimmy Hoffa, the president of the Teamsters Union, was closely linked to organized crime, and Hoffa had been discredited and sent to jail—although, in fact, not much internal change in the Teamsters happened as a result.

There were similar measures that the Justice Department and the Department of Labor could have taken against the UMW and never did. The Labor Department had a suit pending to force the union to obey the Landrum-Griffin Act, and allow election of district officers, but they never pursued it.

In 1968, the UMW endorsed Hubert Humphrey for President—and, it turned out later, supported him with an illegal $30,000 contribution from union funds. When Nixon won the election, however, it didn't hurt the Boyle machine. The Nixon Administration did not have any particular reason to like Boyle, but they respected the union's good relationship with the owners of the coal companies, and they did not want to disturb the status quo.

The first person outside of the union to get involved was a West Virginia Congressman, a rumpled, folksy ex-college professor named Ken Hechler. Hechler had been in Congress for ten years. He had never particularly distinguished himself, always played ball with the union, always assumed that the union was doing its job for the miners.

Before the Farmington disaster, Hechler wasn't thinking about attacking the union. Two months before the disaster, he had co-sponsored a mine-safety bill in Congress. It was weak and didn't have much chance of passing anyway, and Hechler was prepared to let it die. After Farmington, he began to wonder if he shouldn't be doing a little more about the problem. While the men were still trapped underground he called an official at the Federal Bureau of Mines to ask how the rescue effort was going. The official seemed to be less concerned with the rescue, or the explosion, than with the possibility that Hechler might make waves.

"Let's not go blaming anyone for this, Ken," the official said.

"It was incredible to me," Hechler recalled later, "that an agency responsible for protecting the public interest should take a point of view favoring production instead of protection. I'd always thought that human life had the highest priority . . . that explosion galvanized me, convinced me that something had to be done."

Hechler immediately wrote a public statement announcing his new dedication to the cause of mine safety, still not realizing just how much of a storm of antagonism he was about to kick up.

> Coal miners don't have to die. In a civilized society, it is nothing short of criminal to allow the present conditions to continue in the coal mines. Federal and state mine-safety laws are weak, most coal companies seem to know when the inspectors will appear, enforcement of safety standards is weak and entangled in red tape, the union leaders seem more interested in high wages than in health and safety, there is no aggressive attack on the health hazards of coal dust which cause black lung, the coal miners and their families have been steeled to

take a fatalistic attitude toward death and injury and both Congress and the general public have been complacent and apathetic.

From Monongah to Mannington, the same script is grimly familiar. The national searchlight is focused on a disaster. The company officials promise that everything possible is being done. The families wait stoically. The union leaders say that everything possible is being done. The surviving coal miners and their sons say that of course, they will go back into the mines. Soon everybody goes back to the status quo until the next disaster strikes in the coal mines.

Coal miners have a right to live, to breathe, and to be protected by twentieth century safety standards. The nation must rise up and demand that strong and effective mine-safety legislation be passed by Congress.

Hechler came from a coal district, and counted on union support for his Congressional campaign. When he made his statement, he was criticizing the judgment of the union in regard to mine safety, although he hadn't intended to make a direct, all-out attack.

However, the union leaders, particularly Tony Boyle, interpreted his statement that way. They tried to get Hechler to back down, he refused. He was serious in his commitment to safety for the miners.

At the same time, consumers' rights advocate Ralph Nader became outraged about safety conditions in the mines; and he had no illusions at all about the good faith of the union. Nader had become famous as a defender of the rights of ordinary citizens against big business. His first book, *Unsafe At Any Speed*, told how the big auto manufacturers had sacrificed safety—and human lives—

for profit by letting cars go out on the road even though
they had not been properly designed or tested for safety.
General Motors, the biggest auto company, had tried to
discredit Nader by hiring private detectives to follow him,
but when they failed to find any incriminating evidence,
they hired prostitutes to try to involve him in a sex scandal.
Neither tactic worked, and when the detectives were caught
and exposed, the auto companies themselves were discredited.

From the auto industry Nader had gone on to found an
independent group of consumer-protection activists which
got involved in a variety of causes. In 1968, Nader had begun to investigate not only health and safety in the mines,
but also the abuses related to the Welfare and Retirement
Fund.

Simultaneously, a few doctors were starting to raise a
public outcry about a disease which had crippled and
killed thousands upon thousands of miners, and yet had
never been officially recognized as a disease, so that miners
could not claim workmen's compensation benefits for it.
That disease was miner's pneumoconiosis, or black lung
disease, which is caused by inhaling coal dust. Black lung
had always been a problem for miners, but the new continuous mining machines made it even more of a problem,
because of the tremendous increase in the amount of coal
dust, spewed forth by the machines, into the air that the
miners had to breathe.

The symptoms of the disease were graphically described
by Dr. Lorin E. Kerr in a speech at the 1968 UMW convention in Denver.

> At work you are covered with dust. It's in your hair,
> your clothes and your skin. The rims of your eyes
> are coated with it. It gets between your teeth and

you swallow it. You suck so much of it into your lungs that until you die you never stop spitting up coal dust. Some of you cough so hard that you wonder if you have a lung left. Slowly you notice that you are getting short of breath when you walk up a hill. On the job, you stop more often to catch your breath. Finally, just walking across the room at home is an effort because it makes you so short of breath.

In England, black lung had been recognized as an occupational disease of miners since 1942, and workman's compensation had been given for it. But in America, the government officials and the union officials refused to believe that the problem existed. They went on saying that coal dust was not at all harmful.

Another disease, silicosis, or miner's asthma, had long been recognized. Silicosis comes from inhaling rock dust, and it has much the same symptoms as black lung, which comes from coal dust. But silicosis can be detected with an X-ray, and black lung can not until it reaches its most advanced stage, usually right before death. When a miner came down with the symptoms of black lung, doctors on the state compensation boards would tentatively diagnose it as silicosis. Then they would X-ray the miner, and report that the disease had not advanced far enough to qualify the miner for compensation benefits and dismiss his symptoms as fake.

Three West Virginia doctors—I. E. Buff, Donald Rasmussen, and Howley A. Wells—all of whom had been working separately on getting black lung recognized as a serious problem, got together and formed an organization, Physicians for Miners' Health and Safety, and began lecturing to groups of miners throughout the state.

They got an enthusiastic reception wherever they went, and the more graphic and gruesome their presentation, the more the miners responded. Dr. Buff used to come to the lectures with a blackened human lung from a miner's body that had been cut open for an autopsy, wrapped in a plastic bag. Wells would hold up a small section of lung tissue, then crumble it into dry, blackened dust and let it fall from his hand, saying, "Here is a slice of one of your brothers' lungs!" That demonstration would always bring a tremendous response from the audience, particularly when he followed it with: "Where has your union been all this time?"

The miners were finally beginning to realize how little their union was doing for them. Boyle and the Washington headquarters of the UMW had done absolutely nothing to try to get black lung recognized as an occupational disease. The union leaders treated the issue of black lung as beneath their notice.

As 1969 began, the doctors, Ken Hechler, and Nader began to get together in a concerted effort to promote mine health and safety themselves, since it was obvious that the UMW would do nothing. With the encouragement of Buff, Rasmussen, and Wells, a group of West Virginia miners formed a group to press for passage of a black-lung compensation bill in the state legislature. They called themselves the Black Lung Association, and on January 26, 1969, they held a large rally in Charleston, West Virginia, and invited Nader to speak.

Nader was not able to appear, but he wrote a speech and asked Hechler to read it. It was a sharp and detailed criticism of Tony Boyle. Hechler then added his own comment on the commitment of the UMW to health and safety. It wasn't as detailed as Nader's, but it was graphic, and the miners howled with delighted agreement as he brandished a 12-pound hunk of baloney in the air.

Over the next few months, hundreds of miners joined the Black Lung Association. Among them was Arnold Miller, a working coal miner. He did not have black lung himself, as far as he knew, but he cared deeply about what happened to his fellow miners.

Miller was born in 1923, in the tiny hamlet of Leewood in the Cabin Creek section of West Virginia. He started working in the mines when he was 16. He fought in Europe and North Africa in World War II, and was badly wounded—half his face had been shot away, and it took two years and 19 operations in military hospitals to restore it—but then he came back to the mines. He left briefly to become an auto mechanic, but he was back to the mines for good in 1951.

Miller was born three years after John L. Lewis became president of the UMW, and he grew up and began working in the mines during Lewis's great organizing drives of the Thirties. He was of the generation that had grown up with the Lewis presidency—fought under it, and grown comfortable under it. Miller had seen the mine workers become the best paid of all industrial workers, with the best benefits; and he had seen them fall behind the other tradesmen like steel workers and auto workers, as the union stopped fighting for them.

Like most miners of his generation, he believed in his union. But he knew it was autocratic, and like many others he had no particular respect for Tony Boyle. He had joined the Black Lung Association because he realized the union was not doing enough, and he wanted to get the West Virginia workmen's compensation board to recognize black lung as an occupational disease.

In 1970, Miller discovered that he had black lung himself. He had also developed a bad case of arthritis from working in wet mines, and he had to retire. He became president of the Black Lung Association, and discovered that he had a talent for organizing. He orchestrated wildcat strikes and marches on the state capitol, calling attention to his cause with the finesse of a skilled labor organizer.

Tony Boyle and the union reacted to the growing strength of the Black Lung Association with hysterical fury. They charged Miller and his association with "dual-unionism," the charge of setting up a separate union. Miller was shocked by their reaction. Nothing could have made the miners happier than to have the union support them in their bid to get black lung recognized. They didn't want to set up a separate union, they wanted their own union back again.

Instead, Boyle seemed to think the whole issue was blown up. The UMW Journal branded Nader, Hechler, and Miller as "finks" and urged the miners not to listen to them.

A congressional hearing was held on a new health and safety bill which Hechler had introduced into Congress a week after the Farmington disaster. It was a strong bill. Tony Boyle, testifying for the union, asked for two separate bills, one for health and one for safety. He said that the bills would have a better chance of passing separately, but the opposite was true. It was more likely that the union wanted to allow a weakened safety bill to pass, after which they could bury the health bill. The health bill would have cost the coal operators more money in workmen's benefits, and apparently the union was so used to working with the operators that they automatically took their side. Of course, publicly, Tony Boyle vehemently attacked anyone who dared to suggest that he was not standing up for the rights of the miners.

The people who wanted to change the union now found that they had been given a gift by Tony Boyle that Boyle had never suspected. At the 1964 convention, Boyle had extended the president's term from four to five years. That meant that 1969 was an election year, and 1969 was the year that all the latent criticism of the union leadership was coming to a head.

It seemed clear that, for the first time in more than forty years, if a strong candidate could be found, there was a possibility for a real election fight. Not since John L. Lewis had first assumed the presidency had there been any strong challenge to union leadership.

After some wavering Joseph "Jock" Yablonski decided to run. Yablonski had been head of District 5 in Pennsylvania, one of the few districts to elect its own officers. He was a dedicated union man. Although he despised Boyle, he had always supported him publicly in the past, because he felt that union solidarity was the most important thing. But now he decided that Boyle had to be opposed by someone in the election, and, at Ralph Nader's urging, he agreed to run himself.

Although Yablonski, like Boyle, had spent many more years as a union officer than he had in the mines, he was still close to the miners. His house in Clarksville, Pennsylvania, was always open to them, and miners knew they could come by, sit in the den, and talk about their grievances. Yablonski was no rose-in-the-lapel dandy; he was tough, rugged, and plain-spoken, and he had eyebrows that were almost as bushy as John L. Lewis's.

At the meeting between Yablonski and Nader, when Yablonski finally decided to risk everything by challenging

Boyle, this conversation took place. One man had spent his life in the mines; the other knew the union's problems only intellectually, from the outside.

"If I do run, Ralph, they'll try to murder me."
"Oh, they wouldn't dare."

a question of whether . . . you prefer to
sacrifice the efficiency of your organization
'for a little more academic freedom.
          John L. Lewis

Boyle and his henchmen did everything they could to defeat Yablonski.

The first hurdle Yablonski faced was getting on the ballot. Under the new rule, he had to be endorsed by 50 locals. Fifty does not seem that many, considering that there are over a thousand UMW locals, but Yablonski knew that even with the widespread feeling against Boyle, it was still going to be hard to get those 50.

For one thing, although many miners were angry and dissatisfied with the union leadership, there were a lot more who were content to leave things the way they were. Most people don't like radical change. Throughout almost the entire Watergate scandal, public opinion polls kept showing that although most people thought Nixon was guilty, they didn't want him removed from office. No American president had ever been removed from office. And no United Mine Workers president had ever been defeated for reelection in anyone's memory—few could even remember a challenge for the presidency.

Another problem was the way that the local unions were organized. The union's constitution said that every local had to have at least ten working miners in it, but this by-law had been completely ignored over the years, and there were—even by the union's own count—566 "bogus" locals with less than ten working miners. (This figure came to light when the union's records were subpoenaed by Congress in 1971.) These bogus locals were made up of old men on pensions, living in areas where the mines had closed down. They were loyal to the memory of John L. Lewis and out of touch with current problems. They could be counted on to vote the Boyle ticket—especially after Boyle forces spread the lie that Yablonski wanted to abolish their pensions. There were a few pensioners' locals that supported Yablonski, but these were suddenly abolished for having less than ten active miners on their list and being in violation of the union constitution. The other hundreds of bogus locals that were loyal to Boyle were, of course, allowed to stand.

And then there was intimidation, and flagrantly illegal campaign practices. For example, in Girardville, Pennsylvania, where support for Yablonski was strong, the nominating meeting was called for six P.M. Boyle's supporters got there early, nominated Boyle, then set the clocks ahead. When the Yablonski men arrived, a clear majority, they were told they were too late and the nominations were closed. In other locals, the whereabouts of the nominating meetings were a secret to all but Boyle's supporters.

Miners were physically intimidated, and union money was used to bribe local officials to support Boyle and to bribe miners to vote for Boyle. Boyle's campaign trips were billed as "health and safety" speeches, and they were paid for out of union funds.

The *United Mine Workers Journal*, the only publication that many miners ever read, brought nothing but Boyle propaganda to the miners. Throughout the whole campaign for the nomination, the *Journal* never mentioned Yablonski's name and candidacy.

Finally, there was a direct physical attack on Yablonski. On June 28, in Springfield, Illinois, a man rushed out of the crowd and hit Yablonski on the back of the neck, knocking him unconscious. Doctors said it was a karate chop delivered by an expert, coming within half an inch of crippling Yablonski for life.

Despite the obstacles, by August 9th, when the nominations closed, Yablonski had the endorsement of 96 locals.

As the 1969 campaign started, Yablonski hoped to get an endorsement from Lewis. The old man's contempt for Boyle, and his anger at the way Boyle and his cohorts were destroying the union, were well known. "Let them drown in their own slime," he had said when once asked to use his prestige to help Boyle and his friends.

But on June 11, 1969, John L. Lewis died in his sleep, at the age of 89. Lewis's death was a stroke of luck for Boyle, because it meant that Lewis definitely could not endorse Yablonski, although it is entirely possible that he would not have anyway.

And Lewis's death had a tremendous emotional effect on most miners, which Boyle was able to turn into publicity for himself as "John L. Lewis's chosen heir."

There was a third way that Lewis's death benefited Boyle. It was not so obvious on the surface, but it was the luckiest stroke of all, and Boyle wasted no time in taking advantage of it. With Lewis dead, Boyle was able to take over the one position that Lewis still held: trustee of the Welfare Fund.

Boyle immediately had himself appointed to the post. Then, on June 23, he met with George Judy, the trustee representing the coal operators. Boyle told Judy he had a proposal for Judy to vote on, but he told Judy it was only a formality. Ms. Roche had already voted Yes, and her vote and Boyle's were enough to carry the proposal, which was to immediately raise the retired miner's pensions from $115 to $150 a month.

Judy went along with the formality and voted for the proposal, just for the sake of making it unanimous. But it was his vote that carried it. Boyle had blatantly lied about Josephine Roche's vote. She had never heard of the proposal, and she didn't for several weeks. The fund could not afford to pay pensions of that size, but Boyle knew he could count on a lot of votes if he announced the raise. He told Ms. Roche he would rescind the raise after the election, when he was securely in power. Ms. Roche was furious, but she went along with Boyle, out of loyalty to union leadership.

Meanwhile, Jock Yablonski was not campaigning very hard. He had expected that Ralph Nader, who had convinced him to run, would support his campaign. But Nader was involved in other consumer issues—food additives in hot dogs, for instance. Nader felt that he had done his job in acting as a catalyst, and he had never intended to devote his energies to the union election.

Then, too, Yablonski seemed morbidly afraid of getting killed. He often spoke of it, and with Nader's withdrawal, he felt betrayed and alone.

But in reality he was not. His family—wife Margaret, sons Ken and Chip, and daughter Charlotte—supported him one-hundred percent, as did numbers of miners. He met men who were idealistic, committed, and ready to work tirelessly for the cause of freeing the union from dictatorship. The closer Yablonski came to the miners who supported him, the stronger and more committed he became to his own campaign.

And although Nader was no longer involved in the

campaign, Yablonski still had some outside supporters. The chief of these was Joseph L. Rauh, a Washington lawyer who had fought hard and successfully for many social causes, and who had agreed to represent Yablonski in the campaign. Rauh was a busy man, but when Yablonski first asked him to take the job he said, "If you came into my office as a paying client, I couldn't take you. But if you're ready to fight to clean up this union, then I'll represent you."

Rauh committed himself to trying to get a fair election for Yablonski. Rauh's first suit—which he won—was over the firing of Yablonski from his position as head of the union's Washington lobbying organization, Labor's Non-Partisan League. Yablonski was fired as soon as he announced his candidacy, and Rauh was able to prove that the firing had been ordered for political reasons. The court ordered the union to return Yablonski to the job.

As Rauh heard more and more reports like the clock trick at nominating meetings, and the karate chop at Yablonski's head, he tried to get Secretary of Labor George Shultz to step in. In July, during the nominating campaign, Rauh sent Shultz four different letters, each one listing election violations in detail, many of them backed by affidavits from people who had witnessed them. Rauh's first two letters listed 30 separate violations. He described Boyle's "reign of terror," and asked the Labor Department to investigate Boyle for "massive violations" of the Landrum-Griffin Act. Rauh pointed out that the act gave the Secretary of Labor the power to investigate if he thought that "any person has violated or is about to violate any provision" of the act.

Shultz, a Nixon appointee, admitted that it was true that he could, under the law, investigate at any time, even before the election, but he said it had never been done, and he was not going to do it in this case.

Rauh argued that evidence of crooked voting was easy to destroy and that if Shultz waited until lawsuits were filed after the elections, all evidence might be gone. Furthermore, action by the Labor Department before the election might scare the Boyle forces enough to keep them from further violations. Rauh reminded Shultz there had already been a vicious attack on Yablonski and if nothing were done, there could be more violence.

None of Rauh's arguments made any difference. The Labor Department remained uninvolved. Rauh made several more unsuccessful appeals, right up until the week of the election in December.

But Rauh had slightly more success in the courts than with the Nixon administration. In October, a Federal judge ordered the *UMW Journal* to stop acting as a campaign instrument for Boyle.

Later that month, it was brought out in another Federal court that although the union had fewer than 200,000 members, they had printed up 275,000 ballots. Secretary-Treasurer Owens had all sorts of explanations for this in court, none of which were as plausible as the obvious one— the possibility of ballot-box stuffing. All but 51,000 ballots had already been sent out, but the judge ruled that the remaining ballots could not be used.

He also ruled that the Yablonski forces had to be allowed to have an observer at each polling place, an order that was hard to enforce. The Boyle people did not directly forbid Yablonski pollwatchers at the polling places; they just refused to tell the Yablonski organization where the polling places were, and when the voting would be at each of them.

There were other lawsuits, too, started by Yablonski or inspired by his campaign. In August, a $75 million lawsuit was filed by 78 miners and widows of miners, joined by an organization called Disabled Miners and Widows, Incorporated. The defendants were the union, the Welfare Fund, the National Bank of Washington, and the Bituminous Coal Operators Association, and the charge was "willfully defrauding" the miners and their families.

On December 4, five days before the election, Rauh filed an eight-million-dollar suit in the names of Yablonski and 11 other union members against the officers of the UMW. The suit charged that Boyle and company were responsible for massive mismanagement of the union, misappropriation of union funds, nepotism, high living, personal glorification of officers, waste of union money to preserve the political status of Tony Boyle, and unlawful use of union money in the election campaign itself. The damages asked for in the suit were to be paid back into the union treasury.

This last lawsuit was overlooked by a lot of people, coming as it did so close to the election, but it turned out to be very important in the defeat of the abusive union hierarchy, as were all the anti-union lawsuits brought by Rauh.

In the last few weeks before the election, union headquarters released a flood of Boyle propaganda, none of which was as effective as his decision to raise the monthly pension.

Election Day was December 9. It became clear early in the counting that Boyle was going to win. The final tally showed Boyle, 81,056; Yablonski, 45,872. Interestingly, if one figured that Boyle won 90 percent of the pensioners' votes—which is a pretty safe assumption—that in itself would account for his margin of victory, since there were about 70,000 pensioners voting. Even assuming it was an honest election, Yablonski held his own among the working miners.

But, of course, it was not an honest election. Within a few days after the balloting was finished, Chip Yablonski had an affidavit listing 86 separate examples of fraud, intimidation, and vote stealing. For example:

> At local 7962 (in West Virginia) no notices of election were mailed to members, but an observer saw . . . coal operators voting in the union election.

> At local 975 (Pennsylvania) the president of the local marked 25 ballots himself.

> . . . those who appeared at the polls were not afforded the right to vote in secret. They had to cast their ballots in front of the tellers. . . .

> . . . District Official R. Runyon picked up the ballots and put them in his car . . . a Yablonski observer was physically ejected from the polling place.

The list went on. On December 13, Rauh sent a telegram to Shultz citing all these violations and asking that the ballots be impounded, which is a standard procedure in any election where there is reason to believe that there has been dirty work. Shultz did not reply in person, but had an assistant write a letter to Rauh turning down his request, telling him there was not enough evidence to suspect any wrongdoing.

On December 31, three weeks after the election, at one o'clock in the morning, three men drove up to the Yablonski farmhouse. Their names were Paul Gilly, Claude Vealey, and Aubran "Buddy" Martin. They cut the telephone lines leading into the house, and then disabled the two Yablonski cars so nobody could use them to go for help. Then they went into the house.

The Yablonskis had a puppy, Rascal, but he was too little to be a good watchdog; he never barked. Besides, he knew the men. They had fed him hamburger and made friends with him when they had broken into the house to case it a few weeks earlier, when no one was home.

This time they knew that Jock, Margaret, and Charlotte were at home and asleep. They walked upstairs quietly. One of the men went to Charlotte Yablonski's room; the other two took the master bedroom where Jock and Margaret were sleeping. Then they started shooting. Charlotte was shot twice in the head; Margaret was shot in the arm and the chest. They both died instantly. Jock Yablonski was hit with six shots.

After that the house was very quiet for five days, until Ken Yablonski, worried because he couldn't reach his parents by phone, stopped by and found his mother, father, and sister dead.

11 : Reformers' Sweet Victory

. . . struggle and lose, struggle and win
Mother Jones

It was hard to understand why Jock Yablonski was killed after he had already been defeated for the presidency of the union. One would have thought that by then, at least, he would have been safe, no longer a threat.

The murder, though, was more than just revenge for what Yablonski had done. He was still very much a threat to the heads of the United Mine Workers union defeated or not. Of course, his candidacy had been the major part of the threat. The men who had killed him had been hired months earlier, in the thick of the campaign, but up until December 31, they had bungled the job.

Nonetheless, superficially at least, his murder removed a major threat to the union. The lawsuits started by Yablonski could have caused the whole union hierarchy to come tumbling down, and with Yablonski's death, the lawsuit might be dropped.

However, in the long run, Yablonski's death marked the end of Tony Boyle. The murders made headlines across the nation, and while at first threat of libel kept reporters from publicly blaming the union, everyone could read the implication. Millions felt in their hearts from the moment the bodies were discovered that the union was responsible.

Nobody mentioned Tony Boyle's name at first—not aloud, not in public. Ken and Chip Yablonski wanted to, but Rauh talked them out of it. Instead, they issued this public statement:

Our father, mother and little sister are dead. They were shot to death while they slept by professional assassins whose sole intent was to kill them. There was no doubt that these horrible misdeeds are an outgrowth of our father's most recent bid to win election to the [union] presidency.

While many close associates of Yablonski's were frightened, they were also terribly angry. The day after the bodies were found, more than 20,000 men in the mines of Yablonski's home territory, southwestern Pennsylvania and eastern Ohio, stayed away from work.

Ken Yablonski knew how the miners felt. At the funeral, after the Monsignor had spoken, Ken got up and told the mourners; "My brother, Chip, and I would like to carry my father to the grave, but we will carry our mother and our cousins will carry our sister. We will entrust our father to the coal miners he loved so much."

A meeting was held right after the funeral. Mike Trobovich, a union miner who had been one of the strongest workers in the Yablonski camp, said openly that the UMW had killed Yablonski. "Jock knew his life was in danger," Trobovich told a reporter. "He said to me once, 'If anything happens, keep the movement together.' That's what we're going to do."

Joseph Rauh told the miners at the meeting that three weeks before the murders Yablonski and 11 others had filed an $18 million suit against the union, charging that its officers had squandered UMW funds. Rauh offered to carry on the suit if the miners still wanted it. Their response was immediate and positive. "All right, then," said Rauh, "the rebellion goes on."

What happened to the murderers of Jock Yablonski was now in the hands of the police and the FBI. It would only

be a matter of days before they found Gilly, Martin, and
Vealey; it would be several years before the chain of orders
was followed all the way back, and the final verdict brought
in on the man who was behind it all. However, what happened to the union was in the hands of the miners.

There were outsiders who helped. Some, like Congressman Hechler, had been helping all along. Others were
shocked into action by the murder.

The Senate's Labor Subcommittee, chaired by Senator
Harrison Williams of New Jersey, began hearings in February 1970, just a month after Yablonski's murder. Finally,
this subcommittee became interested in Welfare Fund irregularities and the way the UMW election had been run.

George P. Shultz, the Secretary of Labor, also decided at
last that there were enough grounds for looking into the
election. He told Williams's subcommittee on May 4 that
he was convinced that his decision not to get involved
earlier in the election was "a sound one," although he admitted under questioning that he had not investigated any
of Yablonski's charges before making his decision not to get
involved. He also maintained that there was "no evidence
that the murders were connected with the election," although by May 4, Silous Huddleston, a UMW union official, had been indicted on a charge of hiring the three killers. Nonetheless, after Yablonski's death, Shultz did send
out 200 investigators to check into the accusations Yablonski had made about irregularities in the election.

Others who might have been expected to help, still did
nothing. Mike Trobovich sent a telegram to George
Meany, president of the AFL-CIO. It read: "Corruption
and tyranny of UMW now a matter of public record. We
wish to send delegation to enlist aid of AFL-CIO executive council in cleaning up UMW. Please advise when

meeting can be arranged." Even though the UMW was not a member of the AFL-CIO, Trobovich expected they would help in the spirit of unity.

Meany never replied. The reformers were on their own as far as organized labor was concerned. So, in the end it was up to the miners. If they did not have the courage to help themselves, it wouldn't matter what anyone else did to help them.

On April 1, 1970, after a memorial service for Yablonski in Clarksville, a group of miners banded together to form Miners for Democracy. They elected Mike Trobovich president. Arnold Miller, who had supported Yablonski, brought the Black Lung Association into the new organization. Together they set about the business of bringing the union back to the miners.

One of their first moves was to support Lou Antal, a Yablonski supporter who had planned to run against Michael Budzanoski for the presidency of District 5, one of the few districts that had always elected its official. Jock Yablonski had been its president for eight years, until forced to resign in 1966 by a Boyle power play. Budzanoski was Boyle's hand-picked man, and defeating him had been one of the goals of the Yablonski movement. Antal could have backed down, but he did not. Instead he said, "We love our union. We are miners inside the United Mine Workers of America. We want to make it a better union, not destroy it. Let us all never forget that as we work to get rid of the Tony Boyles and their crowd!"

The Miners for Democracy supported Antal's campaign to the hilt. While the votes were being counted, they broke into the room and caught Budzanoski's men tampering with the ballots. The evidence was turned over to the Labor Department, which turned the matter back to Budzanoski, telling him to deal with it in whatever way he thought was best. Budzanoski declared that he had won the election, and Antal, with Chip Yablonski helping him, had to start a long, slow court case to have the election overturned.

The Miners for Democracy decided to fight on many fronts—in elections, in the courts, and in the mines. In July, under Miller's leadership, they organized a strike that closed 150 mines to protest the way the new mine-safety laws were *not* being enforced.

Boyle did not regard the strike as evidence that the miners cared about their own safety and wanted their union to care too. Instead of investigating whether the mine-safety laws were being enforced, Boyle set up a commission to investigate the MFD leaders for "dual unionism." However, Trobovich and Miller went to court and got a ruling that MFD did not have to appear before Boyle's commission.

Meanwhile, Boyle's fortress was crumbling. In January, Gilly, Vealey, and Martin had been arrested for murder, and shortly after, Gilly's wife, Annette, was indicted for conspiring in the plot. Then, on February 25, there came the first indictment that connected the union to the killing. Silous Huddleston, Annette Gilly's father, was accused of hiring his son-in-law and the others to kill Yablonski. Huddleston was president of a Tennessee Mine Workers Union local, part of District 19, the tough district that had provided the hard-hatted thugs for Boyle at the 1964 convention. Huddleston was charged not only with hiring the killers, but also with obtaining the money to pay them. Since Huddleston was not a rich man, it was clear to the FBI that the money came from somewhere higher up in the union. They pressed on with their investigation.

In the meantime, on March 5, 1970, Labor Secretary Shultz announced that his investigation had revealed that

Yablonski's allegations were correct. The Boyle administration *had failed* to provide adequate safeguards for a fair election, *denied* Yablonski the right to post observers, *failed* to follow its own constitution, *failed* to give miners a secret ballot, *denied* some miners the right to vote at all by not holding elections at some locals, *punished* miners who voted for Yablonski, and *improperly used* the money of dues-paying miners to promote Boyle's candidacy. Shultz said that the Labor Department was filing suit in Federal court to have the election results set aside and a new election scheduled.

In May, the Senate subcommittee looking into the Welfare Fund found out how Boyle had lied to the coal operators' trustee George Judy about Josephine Roche's vote on the pension increase. They began an investigation of the economic effects of the increase, and found that if it were allowed to stand, the fund would be broke by 1975.

On August 5, Michael Budzanoski of District 5 and John Seddon, one of his henchmen, were charged with falsifying union financial records in order to channel money illegally into Boyle's campaign.

1971 brought no relief for the Boyle regime. In fact, they were besieged by a deluge of court cases against them. On March 1, Boyle and two other union officials were indicted by a grand jury for illegally channeling $49,250 of union money to make campaign contributions to various political candidates, $30,000 of which went to Hubert Humphrey's 1968 Presidential campaign. Boyle was charged with embezzling $5,000 of the union money for himself as part of the deal. The maximum penalty for Boyle, if he were convicted, would be 32 years in jail and a $130,000 fine.

Three days later, on March 4, the National Bank of Washington asked Boyle to resign from its board of direc-

tors. And three days after that, on March 7, Boyle's attempt
to strike back against his attackers was thwarted when a
judge ruled that Miller and Trobovich and others did not
have to appear before Boyle's dual-union investigating committee.

On April 28, Judge Gerhard Gesell handed down his
verdict in the Welfare Fund lawsuit filed in 1969 on behalf
of 78 miners and widows, charging that the UMW had
cheated the miners in their handling of the Welfare Fund.
Judge Gesell ruled that John L. Lewis had conspired with
Josephine Roche and National Bank president Barney Col-
ton to enrich the bank by keeping the fund's money in a
non-interest-bearing checking account. Boyle himself was
not found guilty of participating in the conspiracy, but
Gesell ruled that he had "violated his duty as a trustee" by
his unethical move in forcing through the pension increase.
The union was ordered to pay $11.5 million to the pension
fund, and to get all the fund's money out of the union bank
by June 30. Boyle and Josephine Roche were both ordered
off the fund's board of trustees, and Judge Gesell ordered
that the new trustees invest and manage the fund's money
for the benefit of the miners.

In June, Claude Vealey, on trial for his life, dropped a
bombshell which, though it had no legal weight, focused
public attention on the possible extent of the conspiracy.
Vealey said that Gilly told him "a man named Tony"
wanted the job done. It was hearsay evidence, but the
union's lawyer, Edward Carey, called a press conference to
deny that the man was Tony Boyle.

By the end of the year, Buddy Martin, Claude Vealey,
Paul and Annette Gilly, and Silous Huddleston were all
found guilty of murder in separate trials. All were eventually sentenced to death. Prosecutor Richard Sprague was

pressing for the death sentence in all these cases to scare the culprits into talking, to implicate the people higher up. Sprague did not want to stop until he had gotten to Tony Boyle.

There was still no evidence linking Boyle, or union money, to the murder. Huddleston was a local president, but there was nothing that went beyond Huddleston, and no evidence that Huddleston had been acting for the union. But even without a murder indictment, Boyle had trouble enough on his hands. On March 17, 1972, he went on trial for the $5,000 embezzlement charge, and on March 31, the jury brought in a verdict of guilty.

Twelve days later, Annette Gilly, terrified by the death sentence that had been given to her husband and afraid she was next, agreed to talk. She admitted that she and her father had planned the murder and hired the three murderers on orders of the union. Most of what she had to say was hearsay from her father, but there was one conference that she could testify directly to:

> My father and I went to Bill Prater's house for the specific purpose of asking Prater whether or not, in the event that someone additional to Yablonski were killed, the union would still pay. Prater replied that he didn't care if the whole family or the whole town was killed as long as the job was done.

Bill Prater was a field representative in District 19, a position close to the union hierarchy in Washington. On April 12, he was arrested and charged with conspiracy in the murder of Jock Yablonski.

At the beginning of May, the two assaults on the union came together with a vengeance. On May 1, in Washington, Federal Judge William B. Bryant overturned Boyle's election on the grounds of massive vote fraud and financial manipulation. On the same day, in Pennsylvania, Silous Huddleston finally talked. He named Albert Pass as the union organizer who had asked him to find a killer for Jock Yablonski. Pass was secretary of District 19; he was also a member of Tony Boyle's Executive Board.

On May 24, a Federal judge ruled that all district officers in the union had to be elected by the members in their districts. Boyle's central control over the union was broken.

A few days later, the Miners for Democracy held a convention in Wheeling, West Virginia. Though Judge Bryant had not yet ordered a new election, they knew he would and they wanted to be prepared. They nominated a slate of candidates to run for the union's highest offices. Harry Patrick, a young militant, was chosen as the candidate for secretary-treasurer. For vice president, they chose Mike Trobovich; for president, Arnold Miller.

It was a true workers' ticket, even more than the Yablonski candidacy had been. Yablonski had been a comfortable union officer who had to rediscover his dedication to the miners. Miller, Trobovich, and Patrick had never been union officials. Trobovich and Patrick were working miners; Miller had been in the mines until only two years before. On June 16, Judge Bryant ordered that a new election be held in December, with Federal supervision.

Boyle had already been convicted of embezzling union money, but he had appealed the conviction, and until the appeal was ruled on, he was technically eligible to run. With incredible arrogance, although his co-officers, George Titler and John Owens, dropped off the ticket, he decided to run against Miller.

But it was all over for the old regime. The voting took place during the first week of December, 1972. The vote count began on December 12, with Federal auditors doing the counting. At the end of the first day of counting, Boyle led by 2,000 votes. By the second day Miller had caught up, and the votes for him continued to pile up. When all the votes were in, Arnold Miller was the new president of the United Mine Workers of America. He had won by 14,000 votes.

There was more to the Tony Boyle story as far as the FBI and District Attorney Sprague were concerned, but for the United Mine Workers, his story was over. They had work to do. A few weeks after Arnold Miller's election, a reporter visiting his office pointed out that his clock was seven minutes fast.

"It's been running behind for so many years, it's got to run fast now just to catch up," Miller replied.

Mr. Miller opened so many doors for us
that the men can't cope with it.
                     Anonymous mine worker, 1975

On August 3, 1973, William Turnblazer, president of District 19 but not part of the murder plot, admitted having overheard a conversation between Tony Boyle and Albert Pass in union headquarters on June 23, 1969.

"Yablonski ought to be killed or done away with," Boyle had said to Pass.

Pass replied, "If no one else will do it, District 19 will do it. District 19 will kill him."

Boyle nodded.

On September 9, 1973, Tony Boyle was arrested for the murder of Jock Yablonski. By that time, Miller had been in office for nearly a year, and the union was hardly recognizable.

The first thing Arnold Miller did as President of the UMW was to slash the president's salary from $50,000 a year to $35,000 and get rid of the extra allowance for expenses that had given Boyle $25 a day on top of his salary. He cut other union officials' salaries by 20 percent, and auctioned off to the miners the three Cadillacs that their money had bought for top UMW officials.

Miller took off the iron gate that had barred the entrance to the UMW building in Washington, throwing it open to the miners and to the press. He opened up the *UMW Journal* to a new policy of press freedom, and today it is considered a model of excellence among labor journals. He moved immediately to carry out the court ruling that districts be allowed to elect their own leaders, and started scheduling the elections.

The UMW convention in December 1973 was held in Pittsburgh, back again in coal country. It was Miller's first convention. The meetings ran behind schedule constantly as members debated openly on the floor for the first time in years. It was very different from the days of Lewis.

Miller made his voice heard when he told the miners he would not compromise on safety measures, the issue that had brought him into the battle in the first place.

> Whether safety reduces production or whether it does not, we don't intend to bargain away our lives for a few more tons a day.
>
> The United Mine Workers is going to enforce safety to the letter with no ifs, ands or buts. And if that is not acceptable to some coal operators, they had better find a new way of making a living. Coal miners of West Virginia and Kentucky and Pennsylvania, and in other coal fields, are tired of dying so that men in board rooms of New York and Boston and Pittsburgh can get rich.
>
> Our legal staff will defend your right to walk out of an unsafe mine and will prosecute companies and foremen who violate the mine and safety laws.

Miller's concern with enforcing mine-safety laws had its effect. Under Boyle, mine deaths had averaged 236 a year; in Miller's first year that number dropped to 132. Coal mining remains the most dangerous of occupations, but now the union is really doing something about that problem.

The winter of 1973 was the winter of the great energy crisis, when the oil-producing Arab nations moved to try and shut off the shipment of oil to the Western world. Coal suddenly became a major fuel source, and when Arnold Miller opened new contract talks in 1974, he was negotiating with a booming business.

On March 29, 1974, a frail, pathetic old man, weakened by a suicide attempt, was brought from the Federal Prison Hospital in Springfield, Missouri, to Media, Pennsylvania, where he was to go on trial for murder.

It was a brief affair. All the groundwork had been done in the earlier trials and confessions. On April 11, the jury found W. A. (Tony) Boyle guilty of murder in the first degree.

The decision meant a lot emotionally to many of the union's members and officers, but their real struggle was still with the coal operators—and once again the union was taking an adversary position. Miller knew that the coal companies were doing very well; and he knew they didn't want to cut down production in the middle of a boom. He drove a hard bargain, and the coal operators insisted his demands were excessive and refused to meet them. Finally, Miller called the miners out on strike. The coal operators capitulated. They signed a new contract that called for a pay raise that put the miners back on level with the steel and auto workers. Miller also made the operators agree to a big increase in royalties paid into the Welfare Fund. Now pensions could be raised from $150 to $375 a month *without* endangering the fund. The contract also called for new, streamlined grievance procedures, five days' sick leave a year where there had been none, and strict safety regulations.

And the contract was no longer negotiated in a secret session between the union president and the coal companies. Every miner in the union voted on it, and Miller insisted that the agreement be written in plain language that the workers could understand.

Running a democratic labor union is not easy, and Miller is not having an easy time of it. One of the hallmarks of any democratic institution is that the structure of democracy is more important than the leaders; and as the 1976 union elections came near, Miller was in danger of being voted out.

Many miners feel he has not gone far enough. A huge wildcat strike began on August 11, 1975, and lasted for a full month. The miners felt the terms of their new contract were not being lived up to. Miller took the position that minor disagreements should be solved by arbitration, not by striking. Many miners feel, though, that the operators have not done enough to set up the quick arbitration panels that they had promised.

Miller tried to get the miners to go back to work, and many miners felt that he was working against them. At the height of the wildcat strike, half the miners in the UMW were on strike, and they seemed as angry with Miller as with the operators.

Miller himself was furious with the operators. It seemed like every time there was a dispute with the miners, the operators didn't bother to talk to the workers but instead went to court to get an injunction to force the workers to keep on working.

During the wildcat strike of 1975, a Federal judge ruled that the UMW was not doing enough to get the miners back to work, and fined the union for every day the strike continued. The fine eventually came to $700,000 and the strike only ended when, at the union's urging, miners crossed the picket lines of other miners and went back to work.

During Lewis's day, and even under Tony Boyle, it would have been impossible to imagine half the union going on strike in defiance of its leaders. "Autonomy?" said one official in District 17, where the strike started. "I've fought for autonomy in the UMW all my life. But what I think we need right now is a dictator."

Others felt just the opposite—that Miller was too autocratic, and that the ideals of the rank-and-file takeover were being lost. Mike Trobovich and Miller have had a falling out. Don Stillman, the young, idealistic new editor of *UMW Journal*, resigned in the fall of 1975 to take a position with the United Auto Workers, and many people saw this as a sign of disenchantment. Chip Yablonski resigned as UMW chief counsel to start his own law firm, although he emphasized that he was leaving not because of dissatisfaction with union policies, but only because he thought it was time to go out on his own.

Arnold Miller and the UMW are discovering that democracy is a lot harder to manage than dictatorship. He and the others who took their lives in their hands after the Yablonski murders, who continued to fight and brought democracy back to the mine workers, are heroes of the labor movement. After any election, they may be gone. But that is what makes them heroes.

Epilogue

There never has been much room for heroes in the mines. The rugged gold miner is a romantic figure, but there is no room for the self-employed, independent miner in an industry where the product is valued by the ton, not the ounce. It takes thousands of laborers to keep a mine in operation, and the profit goes to the owners who can supply the necessary money to start a large scale operation.

In the nineteenth century the coal mines were terrible places to work, and they still are places of great danger. Almost from the beginning, miners fought for the right to band together to win more pay and better working conditions.

The union was genuinely a movement for social change. While John L. Lewis was president he brought the miners many benefits, but he took democratic control of the union away. When miners stood up against Lewis and argued that he was violating their union's constitution, Lewis replied, "It's a question of whether you desire to be the most effective instrument or whether you prefer to sacrifice the efficiency of your organization for a little more academic freedom."

Dictators often tell their followers they are offering "efficiency." The fact that Mussolini made "the trains run on time" has become almost a joke code for fascism. Lewis made deals with the owners of the coal companies in the name of efficiency. Boyle suppressed dissent over such issues as black lung disease and mine safety in the name of efficiency.

Lewis confided to friends in the last years of his life that choosing Boyle as his successor was "the worst mistake I ever made." But it was more than just "a mistake." The level of personal secrecy that Lewis maintained concerning union dealings made some of Boyle's financial shenanigans possible. The power that Lewis gave the position of President of the union turned Boyle into a tyrant. When the union officers were finally brought into court on charges of repeatedly, flagrantly violating the union constitution, Secretary-Treasurer John Owens tried to defend the practice by saying they had always violated the constitution.

John Owens was wrong; the union had not always acted undemocratically; it had not always disregarded the rights of its members. It began with optimistic feelings that people can do something about the terrible conditions of their lives if they work together. The most recent chapter of its history proves that people can also do something about the terrible condition of their union if once more they learn to fight together.

The United Mine Workers union began at a time when most other union members had a skill. The miners knew they were unskilled, but they saw the need to organize. Once they were organized the American Federation of Labor was willing to affiliate with them. But "willing" is a passive word. The AFL never had the desire or determination to organize other unskilled workers. It seems fitting that the move to organize all industrial workers should have come from the mineworkers.

The story of the United Mine Workers union has developed two threads: one, the organization, battling to protect itself and bring benefits to its workers; the other, the reformers, trying to change it.

Mother Jones wrote in her autobiography: "The story of

coal is always the same. It is a dark story. For a second's more sunlight, men must fight like tigers. For the privilege of seeing the color of their children's eyes by the light of the sun, fathers must fight as beasts of the jungle. That life may have something of decency, something of beauty—a picture, a new dress, a bit of cheap lace fluttering in the window—for this, men who work down in the mines must struggle and lose, struggle and win."

Bibliography

ALINSKY, SAUL D. *John L. Lewis: An Unauthorized Biography*. New York: Vintage Books, 1970.

ARMBRISTER, TREVOR. *Act of Vengeance: The Yablonski Murders and Their Aftermath*. New York: Saturday Review Press, 1975.

AURAND, HAROLD W. *From the Molly Maguires to the United Mine Workers*. Philadelphia: Temple University Press, 1971.

BRECHER, JEREMY. *Strike!* New York: Simon and Schuster.

BRUCE, ROBERT V. *1877: Year of Violence*. New York: Bobbs-Merrill, 1959.

DULLES, FOSTER RHEA. *Labor in America: A History*. New York: Thomas Y. Crowell, 1966.

HUME, BRIT. *Death and the Mines: Rebellion and Murder in the United Mine Workers*. New York: Grossman Publishers, 1971.

JONES, MARY HARRIS. *The Autobiography of Mother Jones.*
    Chicago: Charles H. Kerr Publishing Co., 1974.

KAHN, KATHY. *Hillbilly Women.* Garden City, N.Y.: Dou-
    bleday and Co., 1973.

LENS, SIDNEY. *The Labor Wars: From the Molly Maguires
    to the Sitdowns.* Garden City, N.Y.: Doubleday
    and Co., 1973.

McGOVERN, GEORGE, and GUTTRIDGE, LEONARD F. *The
    Great Coalfield War.* Boston: Houghton Mifflin
    Co., 1972.

MADISON, CHARLES A. *American Labor Leaders: Personali-
    ties and Forces in the Labor Movement.* New
    York: Frederick Ungar Publishing Co., Inc.

MELTZER, MILTON. *Bread and Roses: The Struggle of
    American Labor.* New York: Alfred A. Knopf,
    Inc., 1967.

TAFT, PHILIP. *Organized Labor in American History.* New
    York: Harper and Row, 1964.

VECSEY, GEORGE. *One Sunset a Week.* New York: Satur-
    day Review Press, 1974.

Index